First World War
and Army of Occupation
War Diary
France, Belgium and Germany

42 DIVISION
125 Infantry Brigade
Lancashire Fusiliers
1/5 Battalion (T.F.)
1 March 1917 - 31 March 1919

WO95/2654/2

The Naval & Military Press Ltd
www.nmarchive.com
Published in association with The National Archives

Published by

The Naval & Military Press Ltd

Unit 10 Ridgewood Industrial Park,

Uckfield, East Sussex,

TN22 5QE England

Tel: +44 (0) 1825 749494

www.naval-military-press.com

www.nmarchive.com

This diary has been reprinted in facsimile from the original. Any imperfections are inevitably reproduced and the quality may fall short of modern type and cartographic standards.

© Crown Copyright
Images reproduced by permission of The National Archives, London, England, 2015.

Contents

Document type	Place/Title	Date From	Date To
Heading	WO95/2654/2 1/5 Bn Lancashire Fusliers Mar 1917-Mar 1919		
Heading	42nd Division 125th Infy Bde 1-5th Bn Lancs Fus. Mar 1917-March 1919		
Heading	War Diary of 1/5 Lan. Fus. From March 1st To March 31st 1917 Vol 2		
War Diary	On Train	01/03/1917	01/03/1917
War Diary	Liercourt	02/03/1917	16/03/1917
War Diary	Hamel	17/03/1917	23/03/1917
War Diary	Buscourt	24/03/1917	25/03/1917
War Diary	Flaucourt	26/03/1917	31/03/1917
Heading	1/5 Lancashire Fusiliers War Diary 1 April 1917 To 31/4/1917 Vol 24		
War Diary	M.4a. Flaucourt	01/04/1917	04/04/1917
War Diary	Cartigny	05/04/1917	07/04/1917
War Diary	Templeux-La-Fosse	08/04/1917	08/04/1917
War Diary	Saulcourt	09/04/1917	09/04/1917
War Diary	Epehy	10/04/1917	14/04/1917
War Diary	Saulcourt	15/04/1917	15/04/1917
War Diary	Peronne	16/04/1917	17/04/1917
War Diary	Eglosier	18/04/1917	23/04/1917
War Diary	Nobescourt Farm	24/04/1917	30/04/1917
Heading	1/5 Lan Fus. War Diary. Vol 25. May 1917 To 31 May 1917		
War Diary	Camp R	01/05/1917	01/05/1917
War Diary	F22d 2.9	02/05/1917	05/05/1917
War Diary	Villers Faucon	06/05/1917	09/05/1917
War Diary	Pezieres	10/05/1917	12/05/1917
War Diary	14. Willows	13/05/1917	16/05/1917
War Diary	Pezieres	17/05/1917	17/05/1917
War Diary	Saulcourt	18/05/1917	18/05/1917
War Diary	Equancourt	20/05/1917	22/05/1917
War Diary	Viller Plouich	23/05/1917	26/05/1917
War Diary	Gouzeacourt Wood	27/05/1917	27/05/1917
War Diary	Ytres	28/05/1917	31/05/1917
Heading	War Diary 15th Battn. Lan. Fus. June 1st 30th 1917. Volume No. 26		
War Diary	Ytres	01/06/1917	04/06/1917
War Diary	Havrincourt Wood P18d 73	05/06/1917	11/06/1917
War Diary	Q 14 b 5.3 Trescault	12/06/1917	15/06/1917
War Diary	Trescault	16/06/1917	21/06/1917
War Diary	Ytres P 26 a 99	22/06/1917	29/06/1917
War Diary	Havrincourt Wood	29/06/1917	30/06/1917
Heading	War Diary of 1/5 Lancs. Fus. For 1/July 1917 31/7/17 Vol. 27		
War Diary	Havrincourt Wood a.7.a.3.4	01/07/1917	04/07/1917
War Diary	Bertincourt P26.A.7.8	05/07/1917	05/07/1917
War Diary	Gommiecourt A23a.	06/07/1917	31/07/1917
Heading	War Diary Of 1/5th Battn. Lancashire Fusiliers August 1917. Vol. No. 28		

Type	Description	Start	End
War Diary		01/08/1917	31/08/1917
Heading	1/5 Lancs Fus 1st September 1917 To 30th September 1917 Vol 29		
Miscellaneous	On His Majesty's Service.		
Heading	War Diary Of 1/5th Battn. Lan Fus. Sept. 1st-30th Vol No. 29		
War Diary	Sheet 28. I.6b Wilde Wood H.Q.	01/09/1917	01/09/1917
War Diary	I 11b.2.5	02/09/1917	04/09/1917
War Diary	Wilde Wood I 6b.	05/09/1917	07/09/1917
War Diary	611C 5.3	08/09/1917	30/09/1917
Operation(al) Order(s)	1/5th. Battalion East Lancashire Regiment. Tactical Order No. 1	03/09/1917	03/09/1917
Operation(al) Order(s)	1/5th. Battn. East Lancs Regt. Order No. 30		
Operation(al) Order(s)	1/5 Bde. East Lancashire Regt. Order No. 31	07/09/1917	07/09/1917
Operation(al) Order(s)	1/5th Bn East Lancas Rgt. Order No. 32	08/08/1917	08/08/1917
Operation(al) Order(s)	1/5th Bn East Lancas Rgt. Order No. 33	15/09/1917	15/09/1917
Operation(al) Order(s)	1/5th Bn East Lancas Rgt. Order No. 34	13/09/1917	13/09/1917
Operation(al) Order(s)	1/5th Bn East Lancas Rgt. Order No. 35	15/09/1917	15/09/1917
Miscellaneous	To Take Over Accommodation In The Dugout From "C" Coy		
Operation(al) Order(s)	1/5th Bn. East Lancs Rgt Order No. 36	17/09/1917	17/09/1917
Operation(al) Order(s)	1/5th Bn. East Lancs Rgt Order No. 36	16/09/1917	16/09/1917
Operation(al) Order(s)	1/5th Bn. East Lancs Regt. Order No. 37	18/09/1917	18/09/1917
Operation(al) Order(s)	1/5th Bn. East Lancs Regt Order No. 38	20/09/1917	20/09/1917
Operation(al) Order(s)	1/5th Bn. East Lancs Regt. Order No. 39	21/09/1917	21/09/1917
Operation(al) Order(s)	1/5th Bn. East Lancs Regt. Order No. 31	07/09/1917	07/09/1917
Miscellaneous		22/09/1917	22/09/1917
Miscellaneous	Lea 10/24		
Operation(al) Order(s)	1/5th Bn. East Lancs Rgt Order No. 32	08/09/1917	08/09/1917
Operation(al) Order(s)	1/5th Bn. East Lancashire Rgt Order No. 33	15/09/1917	15/09/1917
Operation(al) Order(s)	1/5th. Battn. East Lancs. Regt. Order No. 40	22/09/1917	22/09/1917
Operation(al) Order(s)	1/5th. Battn. East Lancs. Regt. Order No. 41	24/09/1917	24/09/1917
Operation(al) Order(s)	1/5th. Battn. East Lancs. Regt. Order No. 34	13/09/1917	13/09/1917
Miscellaneous			
Operation(al) Order(s)	1/5th Bn. East Lancs Rgt. Order No. 26	16/09/1917	16/09/1917
Miscellaneous	1/5th Battn East Lancs Rgt	01/09/1917	01/09/1917
Miscellaneous	1/5th Battn East Lancs Rgt	30/09/1917	30/09/1917
Operation(al) Order(s)	1/5th, Bn East Lancs Regt Order No. 42	28/09/1917	28/09/1917
Operation(al) Order(s)	1/5th, Bn East Lancs Regt Order No. 35	15/09/1917	15/09/1917
Operation(al) Order(s)	1/5th, Bn East Lancs Regt Order No. 36	16/09/1917	16/09/1917
Miscellaneous	Nominal Roll Of Officers On The Strength Of The Battalion	30/09/1917	30/09/1917
Heading	War Diary 1/5 Lan. Fus. October 1st-31st 1917 Vol No. 29		
War Diary	St. Idesbalde	01/10/1917	01/10/1917
War Diary	Wap Refs	02/10/1917	02/10/1917
War Diary	Belgium Sheet 19	03/10/1917	04/10/1917
War Diary	Coxyde	05/10/1917	05/10/1917
War Diary	Furnes 1/46000 Nieport	06/10/1917	06/10/1917
War Diary	Coxyde & Lombartzyde 1/20000	07/10/1917	31/10/1917
Miscellaneous	War Diary Of Nov 1st-30th 1917 Vol No		
Heading	War Diary Of 1/5th Lancashire Fusiliers Nov 1st 30th 1917 Vol No. 30		
War Diary	Canada Camp Coxyde	01/11/1917	05/11/1917
War Diary	Nieuport	06/11/1917	18/11/1917
War Diary	Teteghem	19/11/1917	19/11/1917

War Diary	Wormhoudt	20/09/1917	20/09/1917
War Diary	Le Nouveau Monde	21/11/1917	21/11/1917
War Diary	Longue Croix	22/11/1917	22/11/1917
War Diary	Steen Becque	23/11/1917	26/11/1917
War Diary	Mt Bernenchon	27/11/1917	27/11/1917
War Diary	Le Preol	28/11/1917	30/11/1917
Heading	1/5th Lancashire Fusiliers. War Diary-Vol 31. 1st December 1917-Page 1-3. 31st December 1917		
War Diary	Le Preol	01/12/1917	03/12/1917
War Diary	Cambrin	04/12/1917	09/12/1917
War Diary	La Bassee 36c NWI 1/10000	10/12/1917	10/12/1917
War Diary	Cambrin	10/12/1917	10/12/1917
War Diary	Beuvry	11/12/1917	20/12/1917
War Diary	Sheet 36 Bne 1/20000 Beuvry Sheet 368 N W I La Bassee	21/12/1917	31/12/1917
Heading	War Diary 1/5 Battn Lancashire Fusiliers 1st-31st January 1918 Vol No. 32		
War Diary	Givenchy La Bassee Sheet	01/01/1918	17/01/1918
War Diary	Sheet 36a. SE. Hingette	17/01/1918	17/01/1918
War Diary	Hingette Sheet 36a. S.E.	18/01/1918	28/01/1918
War Diary	Cuinchy Ref 36c NW. La. Bassee	29/01/1918	31/01/1918
Heading	War Diary Of 1/5 Battn Lancashire Fusiliers 1st Feb. 1918 28/2/18 Vol No. 33		
War Diary	Cuinchy Ref. 36c. NW. La Bassee	01/02/1918	08/02/1918
War Diary	Le Preol 36B N.E.	09/02/1918	14/02/1918
War Diary	Houchin 36B N E.	15/02/1918	28/02/1918
Heading	42nd Division. 125th Infantry Brigade. Vol 14. 1/5th Battalion The Lancashire Fusiliers March 1918		
Heading	War Diary Vol 34 Of 1/5 Batt Lancs Fusiliers 1st-31st March 1918 Vol 14		
War Diary	Houchin Camp. Ref. 36B. N.E K.10.C.4.3	01/03/1918	24/03/1918
War Diary	Sapignies Ridge 57C NW. H3 Clebal	25/03/1918	25/03/1918
War Diary	Gomiecourt Ridge	26/03/1918	31/03/1918
Heading	125th Inf. Bde. 42nd Div. War Diary 1/5th Battn. The Lancashire Fusiliers. April 1918 Vol 35		
Heading	War Diary Of The 1/5 Bn. Lanc. Fus. S Vol 35 1-30 Apl 18 Vol 15		
War Diary	Bugquoy	01/04/1918	08/04/1918
War Diary	Vauchelles	09/04/1918	13/04/1918
War Diary	Warnimont Wood	14/04/1918	16/05/1918
War Diary	Commecourt	16/04/1918	30/04/1918
Heading	Appendices.		
Miscellaneous	The Divisional Commander's Speech	12/04/1918	12/04/1918
Miscellaneous	Situation Reports. received from IV Corps.	07/04/1918	07/04/1918
Heading	War Diary 1/5th Bn. Lancashire Fusiliers. For May 1918 Vol 16		
War Diary	Coigneux Ref. Sheet 57d. 19a. 60.40	01/05/1918	07/05/1918
War Diary	J.2.a.2.4	08/05/1918	31/05/1918
War Diary	Couin Ref Sheet 57D J 2a. 8.2	01/06/1918	06/06/1918
War Diary	Sheet 57D N.E. K 19C. 6.0	07/06/1918	13/06/1918
War Diary	Ref. Sheet 57DNE 1/20000	14/06/1918	30/06/1918
War Diary	Sheet 57D N E 1/20000 Bn Hw K In b 70	01/07/1918	02/07/1918
War Diary	Bn HQ J 20a	03/07/1918	08/07/1918
War Diary	Sheet St Dne Bus-les-Arins	09/07/1918	09/07/1918
War Diary	In Support Bonhq Q16a.5.50	10/07/1918	14/07/1918
War Diary	Sheet 57 Dne 1/20,000. Support Colincatts	15/07/1918	15/07/1918

War Diary	Batthq Q1b05. 50	16/07/1918	18/07/1918
War Diary	Sheet 57Dne 1.20000 Bn HQ. K 25a95	19/07/1918	26/07/1918
War Diary	Bn HQ J 22C 55	27/07/1918	31/07/1918
Miscellaneous	Addendum To Scheme Ref. Advancing Order Cibbe	21/07/1918	21/07/1918
Operation(al) Order(s)	1/5th Lancashire Fusiliers Operation Order No. 15		
Operation(al) Order(s)	Rate Operation Order No. 14	17/07/1918	17/07/1918
Miscellaneous	Acknowledge	21/07/1918	21/07/1918
Miscellaneous	March Table "A" Issued in Conjunction With O.O. No. 15		
Miscellaneous	Working Parties Table "B" Issued Information With 1/5th Bn. Lac. Of O.O. No. 15	25/07/1918	25/07/1918
Heading	1/5 Lancashire Fusiliers From 1st August 1918 To 31st August 1918 Volume No. 39		
War Diary	Ref Sheet 57d NE Bn HQ & J22c55	01/08/1918	02/08/1918
War Diary	Bn HQ K20b15.75	03/08/1918	11/08/1918
War Diary	BHQ J 24 d 6085	12/08/1918	14/08/1918
War Diary	BHQ K 25 Coy 5	15/08/1918	15/08/1918
War Diary	Ref. Sheet 57DNE BHQ K 25 Coy 5	16/08/1918	20/08/1918
War Diary	BHQ K 36a78	21/08/1918	22/08/1918
War Diary	Ref Sheet 57d NE BHQ K 36a 78	23/08/1918	23/08/1918
War Diary	BHQ K29 Coy	24/08/1918	24/08/1918
War Diary	BHQ K25a 83	25/08/1918	25/08/1918
War Diary	BHQ L35a83	26/08/1918	27/08/1918
War Diary	Ref Sheet 57c NW & SW	27/08/1918	27/08/1918
War Diary	BHQ G 33c.23	28/08/1918	31/08/1918
Heading	War Diary 1/5th Lan Fus. September 1918 Vol 40 Vol 20		
War Diary	Ref. 57c BHQ M.5.b20.65	01/09/1918	02/09/1918
War Diary	N.1.a.5.5	02/09/1918	02/09/1918
War Diary	N.4.d.6.9	03/09/1918	06/09/1918
War Diary	Ref 57C NWI. 20000. BHQ G 33c14	07/09/1918	22/09/1918
War Diary	Ref. 57C NW& SW 57C NE & SE	22/09/1918	22/09/1918
War Diary	BHQ 122a 05	23/09/1918	27/09/1918
War Diary	Ref 57c SE 1.20000	27/09/1918	29/09/1918
War Diary	BHQ Q4a11	30/09/1918	30/09/1918
Heading	War Diary 1/5 Lancashire Fusiliers 1/10/18-31/10/18 Vol 41		
War Diary	B.H.Q. Q.4.a.1.1	01/10/1918	07/10/1918
War Diary	B.H.Q. R.14.C.	08/10/1918	08/10/1918
War Diary	B.H.G. R.14.C. To M.11.C. (57 B.S.W)	09/10/1918	09/10/1918
War Diary	B.H.9 N.H.b.4.3	10/10/1918	10/10/1918
War Diary	B.H.Q. I.15.b.8.6	10/10/1918	10/10/1918
War Diary	B.H.Q. D.25.c.5.7	11/10/1918	11/10/1918
War Diary	B.H.Q. D.22.b.7.3	12/10/1918	14/10/1918
War Diary	B.H.Q. D.22.b.7.3	15/10/1918	17/10/1918
War Diary	B.IX.9. D.22.b.7.3 To I.4 C 40	18/10/1918	18/10/1918
War Diary	B.H.Q. 14 C.4.0. To D.2.5.c.5.7	19/10/1918	20/10/1918
War Diary	B.H.Q. 7.25.C.5.7	21/10/1918	21/10/1918
War Diary	E.20 a. 66	21/10/1918	21/10/1918
War Diary	B.H.Q. E.20.a.b.6	22/10/1918	22/10/1918
War Diary	B.H.Q. E 14. anlfal	23/10/1918	23/10/1918
War Diary	B.H.Q. D.28.c.66 B.H.Q. I.15.b.3.3	24/10/1918	31/10/1918
Heading	War Diary 1/5 Lancashire Fusiliers 1st November 1918. 30/11/18. Vol 22		
War Diary	B.H.Q. 1.15.d. (Sheet 75. B.N.E)	01/11/1918	04/11/1918

War Diary	B.H.Q. 15. 7.a.8.4. (Sheet 57b.N.W) R.32.d.8.7 (Sheet 51.a.s.e.)	05/11/1918	05/11/1918
War Diary	Sheet 51A.S.E. B.H.Q. R.32.d.8.7. & Sheet 51. M.36.a.8.2	06/11/1918	06/11/1918
War Diary	Map Ref. Sheet 51 B.H.Q. M.36.a.8.2. C.34.a.7.2	07/11/1918	07/11/1918
War Diary	B.H.Q. O.34.a.7.2	08/11/1918	08/11/1918
War Diary	Map Ref. Sheet 51. B.H.Q. O.34.a.7.2	08/11/1918	08/11/1918
War Diary	B.H.Q. P.31.d.8.8		
War Diary	B.H.Q. P.33.a.8.2		
War Diary	Map Ref. Sheet 51. B.H.Q. P.33.a.8.2	08/11/1918	09/11/1918
War Diary	Q.31.a.1.3	09/11/1918	09/11/1918
War Diary	(Map of Ref. Sheet 51) B.H.Q.	09/11/1918	09/11/1918
War Diary	P.29.b.6.7	10/11/1918	13/11/1918
War Diary	(Map Ref. Sheet 51) B.H.Q. P.29.b.6.7	14/11/1918	30/11/1918
Operation(al) Order(s)	1/5th. Bn. Lancashire Fusiliers. Operation Order No. 45	03/11/1918	03/11/1918
Miscellaneous	Special Order Of The Day by Major-General A. Solly-Flood, C.M.G., D.S.O.	04/11/1918	04/11/1918
Operation(al) Order(s)	1/5th Bn. Lancashire Fusiliers. Operation Order No. 46	05/11/1918	05/11/1918
Miscellaneous	O.C. Companies & H.Q.	07/11/1918	07/11/1918
Operation(al) Order(s)	1/5th, Bn. Lancashire Fusiliers, Operation Order No. 40	07/11/1918	07/11/1918
Miscellaneous	O.C. Companies & H.Q.	06/11/1918	06/11/1918
Operation(al) Order(s)	1/5th, Bn. Lancashire Fusiliers. Operation Order No. 7	06/11/1918	06/11/1918
Miscellaneous	Special Order Of The Day Major-General A. Solly-Flood, C.M.G., D.S.O.	11/11/1918	11/11/1918
Heading	War Diary Volume 43 I Decembr 1918 31 1/5. Lancashire Fusiliers.		
War Diary	Map Ref. Sheet 51 B.H.Q. P.29.b.6.7	01/12/1918	14/12/1918
War Diary	Sheet 81/10,000 Valen Ciennes 3.L.45.38. M. of Mur. 1/10,000. B.H.Q. 2.B.25.80	15/12/1918	15/12/1918
War Diary	Map Ref. Mamur 1/10,000 B.H.Q. 2.B.25.8.0 A	16/12/1918	16/12/1918
War Diary	2.D.3.76	17/12/1918	18/12/1918
War Diary	2.F.35.93	19/12/1918	22/12/1918
War Diary	Map. Ref. Sheet Namur 1/100000 B.H.Q. 27 F 35 93	22/12/1918	31/12/1918
Miscellaneous	1/5th. Bn. Lancashire Fusiliers Administrative Instruction	13/12/1918	13/12/1918
Operation(al) Order(s)	Appendix "B" To Operation Order No. 49		
Miscellaneous	Appendix "A" To Operation Order No.		
Operation(al) Order(s)	1/5th. Bn. Lancashire Fusiliers. Operation Order No. 50	14/12/1918	14/12/1918
Operation(al) Order(s)	1/5th. Bn. Lancashire Fusiliers. Addendum No. 1 to O.O. No. 50	14/12/1918	14/12/1918
Operation(al) Order(s)	1/5th. Bn. Lancashire Fusiliers. Operation Order No. 51	16/12/1918	16/12/1918
Operation(al) Order(s)	1/5th. Bn. Lancashire Fusiliers. Operation Order No. 52	17/12/1918	17/12/1918
War Diary	War Diary 1/5th Lancashire Fusiliers Volume 44 1st-January 1919 31st January 1919		
War Diary	Map Ref. Namur 1/100,000 B.H.Q. 27 35 93	01/01/1919	08/01/1919
War Diary	Charleroi	09/01/1919	15/01/1919
War Diary	Map Ref. Namur 1/100,000 BHQ Chapleroi 2F.35.93	16/01/1919	31/01/1919
Heading	1/5 Lan Fus. War Diary 1st Feb 1919 Vol 45		
War Diary	Map Ref Namur 1/100000 B.H.Q. 2F. 35.93	01/02/1919	28/02/1919
Heading	War Diary 1/5th Lancs Fusiliers. 1 March 1919 31st March 1919 Vol 46		
War Diary	Map Ref Namur 1/100000 BHQ. 2E. 7395	01/03/1919	14/03/1919
War Diary	Map Ref. Namur 1/100. 000 BHQ. 2E 73.95	15/03/1919	31/03/1919
Operation(al) Order(s)	1/5th. Bn. Lancashire Fusiliers. Operation Order No. 49	13/12/1918	13/12/1918

(2) WO95/2654

1/5Bn Lancashire Fusiliers

Mar 1917 - Mar 1919

42ND DIVISION
125TH INFY BDE

1-5TH BN LANCS FUS.
MAR 1917-MAR 1919.

VOL.2 - VOL 26 BLUE NO

VOL 23 - VOL 46

COPY 14, 8, 1, 12

CONFIDENTIAL

WAR DIARY

of

[1/5 LAN. FUS]

From March 1st to March 31st 1917.

VOLUME 23

Army Form C. 2118.

WAR DIARY
or
INTELLIGENCE SUMMARY.
(Erase heading not required.)

VOL 23 - Page 1.

Hour, Date, Place	Summary of Events and Information	Remarks and references to Appendices
March 1st 1919 on train	Arrived PONT REMY at station 4.30 p.m. and marched to	John Ref map 62.D.
2nd " LIERCOURT	LIERCOURT, and occupied billets	John
" " "	No change	John
3rd " "	"	John
" " "	No change Church service.	John
4th " "	" 2nd Lt A.O. HOLLICK arrived with riding horse from EGYPT.	John
5th " "	" 2nd Lt C. SCHULTZ reported from EGYPT. Brass vehicles from ABBEVILLE	John
6th " "	" Bn equipped with new rifles. 1.O.R rejoined from ENGLAND	John
" " "	on furlough	
7th " "	No change 2nd Lt xx D.R. HAWKSEY + H.S. PARKINSON arrived	John
" " "	for duty from ENGLAND.	John
8th " "	No change. B.O.R rejoined from H.P.	John
9th " "	"	John
10th " "	"	John
11th " "	" Church service. 1.O.R rejoined S.H.P	John
12th " "	"	John
13th " "	" 2nd Lt F. ST. BARBE + M.G. CLARKE + 2 O.R. S.H.P arrived	John
	PONT REMY in marching order.	John

WAR DIARY
or
INTELLIGENCE SUMMARY.   VOL 23 page 2.

Army Form C. 2118.

(Erase heading not required.)

Hour, Date, Place	Summary of Events and Information	Remarks and references to Appendices
March 14th 1917 LIERCOURT	no change.	Fallen
15th "	Marched to LONGPRÉ, entrained at CORBIE, rkarched to	Fallen Ref 62D.D.5.a+b
"	HAMEL and billetted in huts. 8 O.R. fell out on march	
16th "	no change.	Fallen
17th " HAMEL	Lt. R.W.G.GRANT and Lt. A.W.K.MONEY returned from	Fallen Ref 62D.P.10.a
"	ah[?] at MARSEILLES. 2.O.R's H.	
18th "	No change. 2nd Lieut arrives. 2/Lt A.B.SACKETT and 2.O.R	Fallen
"	to Hdqrs.	
19th "	No change	Fallen
20th "	"	Fallen
21st "	"	Fallen
"	All ranks passed through gas chamber	Fallen
22nd "	Live bomb practice	Fallen
23rd "	" I.O.R's arrived from ENGLAND "	Fallen
24th " BUSCOURT	Marched from HAMEL to BUSCOURT. 11.O.R. fell out on march	Fallen Ref 62G.N.W H.15.6.87

WAR DIARY
INTELLIGENCE SUMMARY

VOL 23 page 3.

Army Form C. 2118.

Hour, Date, Place	Summary of Events and Information	Remarks and references to Appendices
March 25th 1917 BUSCOURT	2nd Lt A. BRIERCLIFFE, reported for duty from ENGLAND	Lekh,
26th " FLAUCOURT	moved from BUSCOURT to FLAUCOURT and commenced road clearing	Lekh, 62cNW H34.G.6.5
27th " "	No change. Working party of 15 officers & 500 OR on clearing roads	Lekh
28th " "	" Baths on road clearing at BIACHES	Lekh
29th " "	do	Lekh
30th " "	do	Lekh
31st " "	Coy. Major EGLUSIER 2nd Lt SCHULTZ appointed Lekh Pt. 62cG.22.a.35	
	No change. Pow. on road clearing at BIACHES	Ohn Rt.
		62cNW H15.6.87

Cy for midar major
Comdg 1/5 Loutm.

2-4-17

1/5 Lancashire Fusiliers

WAR DIARY.
1 APRIL 1917 – 31/4/1917
VOL. 24

CONFIDENTIAL

1/5 Lan Fus Army Form C. 2118.

WAR DIARY
or
INTELLIGENCE SUMMARY.
(Erase heading not required.)

Vol 24 Page 1

Hour, Date, Place	Summary of Events and Information	Remarks and references to Appendices
April 1st 1917. FLAUGOURT. M4a	H.31a. Batt clearing road at BIACHES. Capt H.M. BENTLEY admitted to Fd Amb. Major G. MOWDER & Lt G.H.G. HUNT returned from furlough to ENGLAND.	All map references Sheet 62c. 1/40.000 Edition 1.
2nd " "	No change Lt Col P.V. HOLBERTON proceeded on short leave to ENGLAND.	"
3rd " "	No change	"
4th " "	"	"
5th " GARTIGNY.	Marched from FLAUGOURT 62c. M.4.a. to GARTIGNY. P.36.	"
6th " "	No change	"
7th " "	"	"
8th " TEMPLEUX-LA-FOSSE.	Marched to TEMPLEUX-LA-FOSSE. D 28 d.	"
9th " SAULCOURT.	Marched to SAULCOURT. E 9 d.	"
9th " SAULCOURT.	Marched to EPEHY. F.1.b. and relieved 1/8 Royal Warwick Regt. in outpost line - Battn of left - 2nd EAST. LANCS Regt. Battn on right 1/4 LAN. FUS.	"
10th " EPEHY	Relief completed 2.15 a.m. Slight artillery action on both sides during night. 1. O.R. Killed by H.E. Batt. of left relieved by 1st Bn WORCESTER Regiment at 11 p.m.	"

1/5 Lan Fus

WAR DIARY
or
INTELLIGENCE SUMMARY.

Army Form C. 2118.

Vol 24 Page 2

Hour, Date, Place		Summary of Events and Information	Remarks and references to Appendices
April 11th 1917	FEHY	Nothing to report, took a do quiet	
12th	"	Capt H.M. BENTLEY returned from hospital, and proceeded	taken
		on short leave to ENGLAND. 1.0.R slightly wounded in face.	taken
13th	"	Nothing to report.	taken
14th	"	Relieved in line by 1/6 ROYAL WARWICK. Regt. and marched to	taken
		SAULCOURT. Relief complete 4.30 am on 15th at 10 Rank & file wounded & missing 2	
		E.9a. 1.27 pm	taken
15th	SAULCOURT	Marched from SAULCOURT to PERONNE. 1.0.R. fell out on	taken
		march. Lt Col P.V. HOLBERTON Reported, on short leave to ENGLAND.	taken
16th	PERONNE	Batln finding working parties, clearing roads.	taken
17th	"	Marched from PERONNE to EGLUSIER G.22a.	taken
18th	EGLUSIER	Nothing to report	taken
19th	"	LT.COL. P.V.HOLBERTON re[turned] and 2nd I/C Bde during absence	taken
		of BRIG. GEN' H.C.FRITH.C.B on short leave to ENGLAND.	
		Major G.MULLER resumed command of Batln. Battn training	

1/5 Lan. Fus.

Army Form C. 2118.

WAR DIARY
or
INTELLIGENCE SUMMARY.

(Erase heading not required.)

Vol 24 Page 3.

Hour, Date, Place	Summary of Events and Information	Remarks and references to Appendices
April 20th 1917 ECLUSIER	Nothing to report - Bn Training.	taken
21st "	do	taken
22nd "	do	
23rd " FARM	Bath & Laundry by neds to march to NOBESCOURT K 32.6.	taken
"	Marched to NOBESCOURT FARM. K 32.6.	taken
24th NOBESCOURT FARM	Nothing to report. Major G. MOULDER admitted to Fld Amb.	taken
25th "	No change. Bath, raiding, working parties. Capt A.H. PEACOCK	taken
26th "	returned from HP and assumed command of Bath.	taken
27th "	No change	taken
28th "	"	taken
29th "	"	taken
30th "	Marched from NOBESCOURT FARM to Camp K5 central	taken

Vol 4

1/5 LAN FUS.

WAR DIARY.
VOL 25.

1 MAY 1917.
31 " "

CONFIDENTIAL

Army Form C. 2118.

WAR DIARY
or
INTELLIGENCE SUMMARY.
(Erase heading not required.)

VOLUME 25 / page 1.

Instructions regarding War Diaries and Intelligence Summaries are contained in F.S. Regs., Part II and the Staff Manual respectively. Title pages will be prepared in manuscript.

Hour, Date, Place	Summary of Events and Information	Remarks and references to Appendices
May 1st 1917 Camp R.5.	In camp standing by ready to go into line. Lt G.F.MAINE Yorks. Regt/Mob Force	R5 central Yakın
" 7.30 a.m	Left camp, and relieved 1/5 Dorsets Regt in line. 1.O.R. wounded. Batt. HQ F22. d. 8.9.	Yakın
2nd F22 d 7.9	In line everything very quiet. 1.O.R. killed by shrapnel.	Yakın
3rd "	Nothing to report. 1.O.R. slightly wounded accidental. 2nd Lt E.D. TRISTRAM. to Fd.Amb.	Yakın
4th "	Patrols active - nil. 1.O.R. killed. 3.O.R. wounded. Lt.Col. rejoined from Command of 125 Bde.	Yakın
5th "	Nothing to report. 1.O.R. killed by H.E. Relieved by 1/5 MAN. Regt. 2nd Lt A.D.SAGRETT, and M.G.CLARKE returned from short leave to ENGLAND.	E22 6.9.0. Yakın Yakın
6th VILLERS.FAUCON	In Camp, nothing to report. 2.O.R. to Fd.Amb.	Yakın
7th "	No change.	Yakın
8th "	Lt. H.R. WAUGH and S. NORTH proceeded on short leave to ENGLAND	Yakın
9th "	Marched from VILLERS. FAUCON to PEZIERES. In reserve to Bde. 2 O.R. to Fd.Amb.	(abov. W30. d. 3.2

WAR DIARY or INTELLIGENCE SUMMARY

Army Form C. 2118.

VOLUME 25 page 2

Hour, Date, Place	Summary of Events and Information	Remarks and references to Appendices
May 10th 1917 PEZIERES	Nothing to report.	W.30.d.3.2. (abn)
11th "	B.O.R. to Fd Amb.	
12th "	Moved from PEZIERES to 14 WILLOWS in line. Relieved X.26.c.5.9. (abn)	
13th - 14 WILLOWS	1/8th Lancs Fus. I.O.R. to Fd Amb. Nothing to report. Very quiet, slight artillery action.	X.26.b.5.9. (abn)
14th "	Still in line. Trenches flooded by very violent storm during night. 1 O.R. wounded.	
15th "		
16th "	No change. 1 O.R. sick to Fd Amb. 5. Lt E.E. JENKINS proceeded on short leave to ENGLAND II	
16th "	Relieved by 1/9 Lan Fus and moved back to PEZIERES W.30.d.3.2. (abn) 1 O.R. sick to Fd Amb.	
17th PEZIERES	In billets 125 Bde. Relieved by 6th LANCERS and moved to SAULCOURT. 2 O.R. sick to Fd Amb.	
18th SAULCOURT.	Battalion inoculated in CHAUFFOURS WOOD II. 1 O.R. to Fd Amb.	E.10.b

WAR DIARY
or
INTELLIGENCE SUMMARY

Army Form C. 2118.

VOLUME 25 page 3

Hour, Date, Place	Summary of Events and Information	Remarks and references to Appendices
May 19th 1917 SAULCOURT	Moved from SAULCOURT to EQUANCOURT. Lt R.H.HALL and 10R sick to F'd Amb. 3 B.O.R. fell out on march believed to have been seized through weather being hot and thundery.	E.10.6. fabric
20th EQUANCOURT	Battalion in our canvas 3.O.R to F'd Amb	V19.a.3.8 fabric
21st "	Battalion training and making preparations to go into line. 1 B.O.R. to F'd Amb.	fabric
22nd "	Left EQUANCOURT and relieved 6 OXF.BUCKS Regt in line Batty HQ at 15 RAVINE VILLERS PLOUICH, Derbyshire 8 on the scale, 18 L.F on right 1/7 Lon. L/F. 10R went old.	fabric R19-a.5.5
23rd VILLERPLOUICH	In line nothing to report	fabric
24th "	No change. LT R.W.G.GRANT Killed	fabric
25 "	Relieved by 13th YORKSHIRE REGT.	fabric

Army Form C. 2118.

WAR DIARY
or
INTELLIGENCE SUMMARY.
(Erase heading not required.)

VOLUME 25 page 4

Instructions regarding War Diaries and Intelligence Summaries are contained in F.S. Regs., Part II. and the Staff Manual respectively. Title pages will be prepared in manuscript.

Hour, Date, Place	Summary of Events and Information	Remarks and references to Appendices
May 26.1917, VILLERS PLOUICH	Relief completed till 4.30 am. owing to food that enemy attacked Bn on right. 6.O.R wounded. Moved into Reserve of GOUZEAUCOURT WOOD. 2ndLt P.V. HOLBERTON proceeded on senior officers conference. Capt A.H PEACOCK assumed command.	K.21.W. Q.22.3.4.4
27th GOUZEAUCOURT WOOD.	Moved to YTRES. Brigade in Reserve. 10.R.Fd.Amb.	Q.22.3.4.4 (adm)
28th YTRES.	Battalion under canvas nothing to report.	P.26.a.8.2 (adm)
29th " "	Battalion training	J.26.a. J.26.w. (adm)
30th " "	2nd Lt E.B. TRISTRAM to Fd amb.	
31st " "	nothing to report	

31.5.17

A.H. Peacock Capt
Comdg 1/5 Somt L.I.

CONFIDENTIAL W/5

WAR DIARY of
1/5TH BATTN: LAN: FUS:
2/6
JUNE 1ST – 30TH

VOLUME No: 26.

2H.G.
5 sheets

Army Form C. 2118.

WAR DIARY
or
INTELLIGENCE SUMMARY.
(Erase heading not required.)

Vol. 26. Page 1.

Hour, Date, Place	Summary of Events and Information	Remarks and references to Appendices
JUNE 1ST YPRES	Battalion inspected by Brigadier General 31th at 11 am. The Adjt. Lt. T.A.G. Machin proceeded on short leave to Eng. 2/Lt. J. Coke acting in absence.	All Map References to 57c SE 1:20,000
2ND "	Batt. in training. Lt. R. Hall struck off strength on secondment to Eng.	H.S.P.
3RD "	Church parade – C.O. 2 i/c in Command and M.O. on short Gas Course for the day. 11.30 p.m. false alarm of GAS.	H.S.P.
4TH "	Batt. training. Major G.S. Castle. M.C. 1/5th Batt. Gloucester Regt. joins for duty and assumes Command of the Batt. vice Capt. A.H. Peacock 2 OR to H.Q. Ambl. for Dental Treatment.	H.S.P.
5TH HAVRINCOURT WOOD P18 d 7.3.	Batt. moves to HAVRINCOURT WOOD by march route. Relieved 1/4th East Lancs. Regt. in Right Bde Res. Relief complete by 5 p.m. 2 Companies in INTERMEDIATE LINE Q 8 d 3.7 to Q 8 d 8.1.	H.S.P.
6TH "	200 men are working parties with front Batt. in Right Sector. 1/7 Lan. Fus. 1 OR wounded	H.S.P.
7TH "	Lt. Col P.V. Holberton returns to duty and takes over Command. Major G.S. Castle, M.C., assumes duties as 2nd in Command. Capt. A.H. Peacock takes over command of "A" Coy. vice Capt. G.B. Horridge who reverts to his permanent rank of Lieut. 6 OR to H.Q. Amb. sick. Working parties with front line Batt. and work done on INTER. LINE	H.S.P.
8TH "	No change. 1.40 a.m. alarm of GAS from the front - proves to be false. Working parties found for front line Batt. 2 OR to H.Q. Amb. sick.	H.S.P.
9TH "	No change. Working parties for front line. – 2 OR to H.Q. Amb. sick	H.S.P.

Army Form C. 2118.

WAR DIARY
or
INTELLIGENCE SUMMARY.
(Erase heading not required.)

Vol. 26 Page 2

Instructions regarding War Diaries and Intelligence Summaries are contained in F.S. Regs., Part II. and the Staff Manual respectively. Title pages will be prepared in manuscript.

Hour, Date, Place	Summary of Events and Information	Remarks and references to Appendices
JUNE 10th HAVRINCOURT WOOD P18d 7.3.	Working parties found for front line. 2 O.R. rank wounded by minenwerfer.	A.P. All map references to 57c SE 1:20,000.
11th	Batt. relieved 1/4th LAN. FUS. in RIGHT SECTOR in front of TRESCAULT on A Coy in support. C Coy in B Coy in front line and Sap. N.B. and C respectively. Batt. HQ. at Q 14 b 5.3. 1 O.R. wounded during relief. 2nd LT. C.H. HARRISON proceeded on short leave to ENGLAND.	A.P.
12th Q 14 b 5.3. TRESCAULT	Batt. in line - nothing to report. Batt on right 1/6th NORTH STAFFS. 59th DIV Batt. on left 1/8th LAN. FUS. 1 O.R. sick to 2/3 Amb.	A.P.
13th "	Batt in line. Our patrols active to FEMY WOOD. a fighting patrol consisting of A/LT. C.B. HORRIDGE and 10 O.R. arrived at a successful raid on enemy position in the wood. 1 O.R. killed on the patrol. Casualties inflicted on the enemy. 2nd LT. J.C. LORD slightly wounded. 1 O.R. wounded & returned to duty. 1 to Hospital	A.P.
14th "	In line. Enemy minenwerfers and M.G.s troublesome at night. Our working parties busy connecting Sap Heads by rifle pits.	A.P.
15th "	In line - work on defences progressing well. 2/LT ADJUTANT LT. T.A.G. MASHITER returned from short leave and resumed his duties. CAPT. A.H. PEACOCK proceeded on short leave to ENGLAND. 1 O.R. sick to 2/3 Amb.	A.P.

(73989) W4141—463. 400,000. 9/14. H.&J.Ltd. Forms/C. 2118/10.

Army Form C. 2118.

WAR DIARY
or
INTELLIGENCE SUMMARY.
(Erase heading not required.)

Vol. 26 page 3.

Instructions regarding War Diaries and Intelligence Summaries are contained in F.S. Regs., Part II. and the Staff Manual respectively. Title pages will be prepared in manuscript.

Hour, Date, Place	Summary of Events and Information	Remarks and references to Appendices
JUNE 16th TRESCAULT	Batt. in line. Enemy trench mortars and M.G.s busy at night.	All map references
	1 Sgt wounded on patrol to FEMY WOOD. Batt. forward H.Q. to Q19a44.	1:20,000
	Lt. C.H.C. HUNT returned from 4th Army Infantry School.	M.S.P.
	1 OR severely wounded by Minenwerfer - 1 OR accidental bayonet wound.	
JUNE 17th "	1 OR severely wounded abroaded in Res. Amb.	M.S.P.
	Enemy rifle grenades troublesome. 2 OR killed 2 OR wounded.	
	Lt. ST. BARBE proceeded on short leave to ENGLAND.	
JUNE 18th "	In line. Enemy positions in FEMY WOOD bombed by Infantry	M.S.P.
	patrols and subjected to concentrated M.G. fire in retaliation for	
	his activity with rifle Grenades.	
	Enemy Minenwerfers busy - 3 OR killed 2 OR shell shock and 1 OR	M.S.P.
	wounded and admitted. 1 OR sick to Res. Amb.	
JUNE 19th "	In line. Usual work on safety rifle pits and T's and trenches	M.S.P.
	and M.G. activity against FEMY WOOD. 3 OR sick to Res. Amb.	
" 20th "	In line. Trenches flooded with heavy rain storms.	M.S.P.
	Enemy Minenwerfers shell troublesome at night.	
	1 OR to Res. Amb. and accidental injury to foot.	
" 21st "	Batt. relieved by 1/5th Batt. EAST LANCS REGT. Relief complete at	M.S.P.
	Batt. moved to YPRES by train - under Canvas at Same Camp	
	as before at P.26.a.99	
	1 OR. sick to Res. Amb.	

Army Form C. 2118.

WAR DIARY
or
INTELLIGENCE SUMMARY.
(Erase heading not required.)

Vol. 26. page 4

Instructions regarding War Diaries and Intelligence Summaries are contained in F.S. Regs., Part II. and the Staff Manual respectively. Title pages will be prepared in manuscript.

Hour, Date, Place	Summary of Events and Information	Remarks and references to Appendices
JUNE 22ND YPRES P.26.a.9.9	Batt. under Canvas in rest. Cleaning up and bathing.	All map references to Map. 57c SE 1:20,000.
23rd "	Church parade.	
24th "	Batt. in training and finding working parties. 6 O.R. sick to Fd. Amb.	H.S.P.
25th "	" " Lt. T.A.G. MASHITER proceeded on Course to 4th Army Infantry Sch. 2nd/Lt. J. CARTER assumes duties of Adjt. during his absence.	H.S.P.
26th "	Batt. inspected by Brig. Gen. FARGUS Cmdg. the Brigade in the morning. Afternoon spent at games and sports	H.S.P.
27th "	Batt. training and finding working parties.	H.S.P.
28th "	" "	H.S.P.
29th "	Batt. training. 3 O.R. to Fd. Amb. 10 p.m. Batt moved to Gtd. 3.3. in Brigade Res. with 2 platoons as permanent garrison of the Intermediate line and 2 in the Second line. 1 O.R. sick to Fd/Amb.	H.S.P.
30th HAVRINCOURT WOOD	6 O.R. sick to Fd. Amb. Batt. training and finding working parties	H.S.P.

P.N. Holberton Lieut Col.
Cmdg 1/5 Devon Regt

(73989) W4141—463. 400,000. 9/14. H.&J.Ltd. Forms/C. 2118/10.

95/44

CONFIDENTIAL.

WAR. DIARY

OF

1/5 LANCS. FUS.

FOR

1 JULY 1917
31/7/17

VOL. 27.

WAR DIARY 1/5 LANCS. FUSRS. Army Form C. 2118.

or

~~INTELLIGENCE SUMMARY~~

(Erase heading not required.)

VOL >7. PAGE 1.

Hour, Date, Place	Summary of Events and Information	Remarks and references to Appendices
July 1. 1917. HAVRINCOURT WOOD. Q.7 a.3.4.	Battn in L/6 reserve 16 126 Bde finding working parties by night and day. 2 Platoons permanent garrison of intermediate line. 1 Coy permanent garrison of second Line 1 S. exp. + two L.G.s. 2. Coys firing on miniature range, & working parties.	ALL MAP REFERENCES on THIS PAGE. SHEET 57.c. 1/40.000. JC
2	do	do
3	do	do
4	do	do
5. BERTINCOURT. P26 A.7.8. 6 a.m.	Battn moved by BEAUVOIS at 1 am July 5. to BERTINCOURT >6.A.7.8. in huts & billets preparatory to moving to III Army Reserve. 125 Rees Sports.	JC
6. 5 a.m. do	Battn move by march route to GOMMIECOURT. Ass.c. under Canvas. III Army. VI Corps. Battn in Army Reserve.	
11 am GOMMIECOURT A.28 a. 7 to 31/=.	Battn undergoing progressive training, especially in New formations, & TRENCH to TRENCH ATTACK. Pl. Bde & Bunil Mounted, Dismounted Sports. Boxing competitions.	JC

P.V. Holladay
Lt. Col.
5 Jan 35
Comds 1/5 Lancs Fus.

CONFIDENTIAL.

WAR DIARY
OF
1/5th Battn. Lancashire Fusiliers

August 1917.

Vol. No. 28.

Vol 7

26.G
2 sheets

WAR DIARY or INTELLIGENCE SUMMARY

Army Form C. 2118.

1/5th LANCASHIRE FUSILIERS.

Vol. 28. Page 1

Hour, Date, Place	Summary of Events and Information	Remarks and references to Appendices
Aug 1. 1917	Battn still in rest training in hutments. Bayonet fighting, with platoon & Battn in trench attack. Some night operations & ceremonial parades.	Ref Map 57C N.W. 1/20,000 CA 29 & Central.
16.		
Aug 19 1917 9 a.m.	Battn moved by march route to BOUZINCOURT. Encamped in Jussiers camp.	Ref Map.
Aug 20.	"	"
21	"	"
22. 1 p.m.	" moved by train from ALBERT to GODSWAERSWELDE. Beguim arriving at 1 a.m. where after a short rest for tea again moved by march route to hutments at ref Map Sheet 27. 1/40,000. L.17. central. Watou Area.	"
23, 24, 25, 26, 27, 28	" still in hutments, very little training owing to inclement weather.	"
29. 8.30 a.m.	" moves by march route to POPERINGHE, and from there by train to Much. op. 28 N.W. Sheet H13 a 5.4. whence	"
30. "	" Organising & arranging details of relief of Hatupou [?] 6 in front line moving through D.2.B central, which takes	"
31. "	" place to day about 1.30 p.m. Battn in line, heavy shelling, saw casualties.	"

J.S. Castle Maj
for Lt Colonel
Comdg 1/5 Lan Fus.

125/42

Vol d

1/5 Lmes Fus

1st September 1917.
to
30th "   "

Vol 29.

Copy 11, 7

On His Majesty's Service.

Brigadier General J. E. Edmonds, C.B., C.M.G.,
Historical Section,
Committee of Imperial Defence,
Audit House,
Victoria Embankment,
E.C.4.

T.S. Anspo II & IX
from Sir. Edmonds

THE WAR OFFICE.

Confidential. 65 61/2 Vol 8

WAR
DIARY
of
16th Poona San two."
Sept 1st — 30th. 1917
Vol No 29

full 27.6.
3 sheet

1/5th LANCASHIRE FUSILIERS

VOL. 29. PAGE 1.

Army Form C. 2118.

WAR DIARY
or
INTELLIGENCE SUMMARY.
(Erase heading not required.)

Instructions regarding War Diaries and Intelligence Summaries are contained in F.S. Regs., Part II. and the Staff Manual respectively. Title pages will be prepared in manuscript.

Hour, Date, Place	Summary of Events and Information	Remarks and references to Appendices
September 1st. SHEET 28. I.6.c. WILDE WOOD M.G.	In outpost line in right sub sector of 126th Front from YPRES - ROULERS Railway (inclusive) D.25.d. 65.15. to cross roads (inclusive) D.25.a. 65.75. B Coy on the right. C Coy on the left. A Coy in support at BILL COTTAGE I.6.c.2.8. D Coy in at I.6.a.2.7. 1/6th LAN. FUS. on our right. 21st LONDON REGT. on our right. Moved out night into support relieved by 1/7th LAN. FUS. H.Q. CAMBRIDGE ROAD I.a.6.3.5. C and D Coys go back for General training to H.Q.a. A & B Coys in IBEX RES. TR. M.I.6.a. Heavily shelled by 4.2 in CAPT. A.P. HUDSON & 2nd LT MASHITER killed by rifle.	
September 2nd I 11.6.2.5. 3rd " 4th " WILDE WOOD I.6.6. 6th "	In support. HON. LT. & B.M. WHITTAKER wounded on POT/17F5 ROAD. PRELIMINARY Bombardment with 6 in, 12 in, 7.15 in. Heavy. Preceding barrage on BORRY FARM D.25 & preparatory fire from shells by enemy at night into outpost - 2 bombs - moved into some outpost line at night heavily. Trench dug to attack. In outpost line - 3rd Bn front of BORRY FARM. C & D Coys move into assembly trench at midnight. 7.15 a.m. Heavy bomb. of BORRY FARM. 7-30 a.m ZERO HOUR C.D Coys attack BORRY FARM Behind Creeping barrage. 1/6th LAN. FUS. attack BECK HOUSE and IBERIAN on left D.19 & 1.t. & B. respectively. 6.7th DIV. attack HILL 35 D.19.6 at same hour. Sharp fighting throughout day. Heavy machine gun fire met from VAMPIR and DOS. S.of BORRY and attack held up after 150 yds. Heavy counter attacks at 10-45 a.m. 7-30 p.m. and 11-10 p.m. but up by our artillery fire. At 7.30 p.m our left which was in the air had to retire to the original line. The right succeeded in holding the line D 26 & 25.20.6 D 25 & 15-30 and this Coy consolidated the left being brought back and joined to our original line. In the attack we had heavy casualties from M.G fire on right. CAPT. A.B. JACKETT was wounded in 3 places but Rt to his P.o. on the right. LTS. MORGAN, MURPHY, TRISTRAM & HARRISON are missing. LT. BRIERCLIFFE, BRIGGS were wounded.	

WAR DIARY
or
INTELLIGENCE SUMMARY.
(Erase heading not required.)

Army Form C. 2118.

PAGE 2.

Hour, Date, Place	Summary of Events and Information	Remarks and references to Appendices
SEPT. 7th	In outpost line at night relieved by 1/5th MAN. REGT. came into rest at ST LAWRENCE CAMP. BRANDHOEK area G.11.c.5.3.	
SEPT. 8th G.11.c.5.3	In rest camp	
" 9, 10, 11, 12th	In rest camp, right of 16th moved into support in ibex Res: fixed with H.Q. in CAMBRIDGE ROAD. Relieved 1/7th MAN.REGT.	
13, 14th		
15th	In support	
16th	In support.	
17th	In support — right 9/17th relieved by 1st S.A.I.R. and returned to BRANDHOEK.	
18th	BRANDHOEK	
19th	Moved to JAN-TER-BIEZEN - in Camp.	
20th	Cleaning up and training	
21st	" "	
22nd	Moved to ARNEKE	
23rd	Training	
24th	"	
25th	Moved to GAYVELDE	
26th	Moved to ST IDESBALDIE	
27th	Training	
28th	"	
29th	Route march.	
30th	Sunday, divine service &c.	

Signed
a/ Major
fr Lt Col Chni
1/5 Lan Fus.

SECRET.

Copy No. 12.

F

1/5th. Battalion East Lancashire Regiment.

TACTICAL ORDER. No.1.

Ref. Map, 28,N,W,& N.E. 1/20,000.   3rd. September, 1917.

1. The Brigade Front is as follows :-

   RIGHT BOUNDARY.

   The cross roads J.1.d.6.2. exclusive - South of JAFFA AVENUE - KIEL HOUSE inclusive, except two dug-outs immediately South of KEIL HOUSE - J.7.A.0.7. - I.12.a.85.80.-I.12.a.2.0. -I.11.d.1.5.- I.10.d.7.1. - HELL FIRE CORNER.

   LEFT BOUNDARY.

   The YPRES-ROULERS Railway inclusive as far as HELL FIRE CORNER.

2. This front is held by 1 Battalion with 1 Battalion in support and 2 Battalions in reserve.

   Bde. Headquarters.....RAILWAY WOOD.
   Front Battalion.......Headquarters KIT AND KAT (J.1.d.3.6.)
                         2 Companies in the Front System.
                         1 Company at LAKE FARM (I.12.b.8.9.)
                         1 Company at I.6.d.90.95.

   Support Battalion.   Headquarters RAILWAY WOOD.
                         2 Companies RAILWAY WOOD.
                         2 Companies under canvas YPRES South Area.

   Reserve Battalion.   Under canvas YPRES South Area.

3. DEFENSIVE SYSTEM.

   (a)   Front Line: which consists of detached posts on the forward slope of WESTHOEK RIDGE.

   (b)   WESTHOEK RIDGE: which is the main line of resistance and will be held in all circumstances.

   (c)   BELLEWARDE RIDGE: where two Companies of the Support Battalion are situated.

4. ACTION IN CASE OF ATTACK.

   Front Battalion.:
   The front line will be held in all circumstances,
   In the event of the enemy penetrating our defences, he will be driven out by immediate counter attack organised within the Battalion.
   Garrisons on the flanks of the point attacked will maintain their position until the last, so that the enemy may be held in a pocket, and will assist in the subsequent counter attack by harassing his flanks with fire.

   Support Battalion:
   The two companies of the Support Battalion in RAILWAY WOOD will be at the disposal of the Brigadier, for any of the following purposes :-
   (1) Counter attack on the advanced line of posts.

(2)

-2-

 (2) Counter attack on WESTHOEK RIDGE.
 (3) Occupation of WESTHOEK RIDGE.

  The two companies in YPRES SOUTH will "Stand To" and will be prepared to move forward to RAILWAY WOOD immediately upon the receipt of orders.

Reserve Battalions
  Will "Stand To" and be ready to move up at 10 minutes notice, after the first 20 minutes has elapsed from the receipt of the warning.

5. BATTALION HQRS & 2 Companies will probably move into support in RAILWAY WOOD on the night of the 5/6th, leaving 2 Companies under canvas at YPRES SOUTH.

6. All troops moving into the Line either for the ordinary relief or under Para 4.above will carry two days rations.
  During period that the Battalion is in reserve, the 2nd. day's rations will be kept in bulk by Coy's and issued immediately on receipt of orders to "Stand To". Fighting Dress less greatcoats, Flares. Bombs, Rifle Grenades and entrenching tools (i.e. picks & shovels) will be worn.
 All equipment must be put together at night, ready for immediate use.

             E.Elliott
             Captain & Adjutant
             1/8th. Bn. East Lancs Regt.

Issued by Orderly at......9......P.M.

Copy. No.1. "A" Coy.
" " 2 "B" "
" " 3 "C" "
" " 4 "D" "
" " 5 2nd in Command.
" " 6 Sig. Off.
" " 7 Int. Off.
" " 8 T.O.
" " 9 Q.M.
" " 10. War Diary.
" " 11. " "
" " 12 File.

SECRET.

Copy No 11

1/5th. Battalion East Lancashire Regiment.

TACTICAL ORDER. No.1.

Ref. Map, 28,N.W.& N.E. 1/20,000,   3rd, September, 1917.

1. The Brigade Front is as follows :-

   RIGHT BOUNDARY.

   The cross roads J.1.d.6.2. exclusive - South of JAFFA AVENUE - EIEL HOUSE inclusive, except two dug-outs immediately South of EIEL HOUSE - J.7.C.6.7. - I.12.a.85.50.- I.12.a.2.0. - I.11.d.1.5.- I.10.d.7.1. - HELL FIRE CORNER.

   LEFT BOUNDARY.

   The YPRES-ROULERS Railway inclusive as far as HELL FIRE CORNER.

2. This front is held by 1 Battalion with 1 Battalion in support and 2 Battalions in reserve.

   Bde. Headquarters.....RAILWAY WOOD.
   Front Battalion........Headquarters KIT AND KAT (J.1.d.3.6.)
                          2 Companies in the Front System.
                          1 Company at LAKE FARM (I.12.b.5.9.)
                          1 Company at I.6.d.80.95.

   Support Battalion.   Headquarters RAILWAY WOOD.
                          2 Companies RAILWAY WOOD.
                          2 Companies under canvas YPRES South Area.

   Reserve Battalions   Under canvas YPRES South Area.

3. DEFENSIVE SYSTEM.

   (a)   Front Line: which consists of detached posts on the forward slope of WESTHOEK RIDGE.

   (b)   WESTHOEK RIDGE: which is the main line of resistance and will be held in all circumstances.

   (c). BELLEWARDE RIDGE: where two Companies of the Support Battalion are situated.

4. ACTION IN CASE OF ATTACK.

   Front Battalion :
       The front line will be held in all circumstances.
       In the event of the enemy penetrating our defences, he will be driven out by immediate counter attack organised within the Battalion.
       Garrisons on the flanks of the point attacked will maintain their position until the last, so that the enemy may be held in a pocket, and will assist in the subsequent counter attack by harassing his flanks with fire.

   Support Battalion:
       The two companies of the Support Battalion in RAILWAY WOOD will be at the disposal of the Brigadier, for any of the following purposes :-
           (1) Counter attack on the advanced line of posts.

(2)

(2) Counter attack on WESTHOEK RIDGE.
(3) Occupation of WESTHOEK RIDGE.

The two companies in YPRES SOUTH will "Stand To" and will be prepared to move forward to RAILWAY WOOD immediately upon the receipt of orders.

Reserve Battalions
Will "Stand To" and be ready to move up at 10 minutes notice, after the first 20 minutes has elapsed from the receipt of the warning.

5. BATTALION HQRS & 2 Companies will probably move into support in RAILWAY WOOD on the night of the 5/6th, leaving 2 Companies under canvas at YPRES SOUTH.

6. All troops moving into the Line either for the ordinary relief or under Para 4, above will carry two days rations.
During period that the Battalion is in reserve, the 2nd, day's rations will be kept in bulk by Coy's and issued immediately on receipt of orders to "Stand To". Fighting Dress less greatcoats, Flares. Bombs, Rifle Grenades and entrenching tools (i.e. picks & shovels) will be worn.
All equipment must be put together at night, ready for immediate use.

Captain & Adjutant
1/5th, Bn, East Lancs Regt.

Issued by Orderly at....9.....P.M.

Copy. No. 1. "A" Coy.
" " 2 "B" "
" " 3 "C" "
" " 4 "D" "
" " 5 2nd in Command.
" " 6 Sig. Off.
" " 7 Int. Off.
" " 8 T.O.
" " 9 Q.M.
" " 10. War Diary.
" " 11. " "
" " 12 File.

SECRET.   Copy No. 11.

1/5th. Battn. East Lancs Regt. Order No. 30.

Ref. Map. Sheet 28 N.W. & N.E.

1. (a) The 1/10th. Bn. Manchester Regt. has been ordered to relieve the 1/4th. Bn. East Lancs Regt. in the Front Line on the night of the 5/6th. September, 1917.

   (b) Hdqrs. "B" & "D" Coy's of this Battalion will replace "Hdqrs." "A" & "B" Coy's 1/10th. Bn Manchester Regt. in RAILWAY WOOD in Brigade Support.

   (c) "A" & "C" Coy's of this Battalion under Captain F. BRITCLIFFE will remain in camp at YPRES SOUTH also forming Brigade Support.

2. "Hdqrs" "B" & "D" Coy's will proceed in the above order from present camp at 8-30 p.m. by KRUISSTRAT, WARRINGTON ROAD (Corduroy Road, South of YPRES.) GORDON HOUSE to vicinity of BIRR Cross Roads.
   Head of column to reach BIRR CROSS ROADS 10-10 p.m. where guides will meet.

3. Dress for marching out. :-
   Fighting dress, less greatcoats, flares, bombs, rifle grenades and entrenching tools (i.e. picks and shovels.)
   The following will be carried in the pack.:-
   Groundsheets, cardigan, one pair of socks, two day's rations plus the emergency ration, one solidified alchol refill for "Tommies Cooker" per 3 men.
   170. Rounds of S.A.A. per man will be carried, the extra 50 rounds per man being issued to the whole Battalion from mobile reserve.
   Three Petrol Tins per Platoon and one Petrol Tin per Coy Hdqrs will be carried empty for use in RAILWAY WOOD.

4. 4. Lewis Guns per Coy, and 24 Magazines per gun will be taken forward on Pack Animals, one Pack Animal per Lewis Gun which will carry in addition 24 magazines and spare part bag.
   Each pack mule will proceed with its platoon as far as a point on the Corduroy Road about I.17.a.85. - 90.
   before Corduroy Road runs into the MENIN ROAD about 200 yards W. of BIRR Cross Roads.
   At this point they will be unloaded and man-handled forward.
   Pack mules will rendezvous here and return after all platoons have past.

5. "B" & "D" Coy will each detail one Officer and 5.O.R. (1.Sgt.) to proceed to RAILWAY WOOD and report to the Adjutant 1/10th. Bn. Manchester Regt. by 4-0 p.m., they will find out exact position of all dugouts which their Coy's are to occupy in RAILWAY WOOD.
   Officers who proceeded to RAILWAY WOOD yesterday will not be sent as they are required to guide their Companies to BIRR Cross Roads at night.

6. Distances of 100 yards between half platoons will be maintained on leaving this camp for move forward, half platoons proceeding in file, special attention must be paid to keeping touch between half platoons.

7. All surplus kit of "Hdqrs" "B" & "D" Coy's to that being carried in packs will be packed in Haversacks, except greatcoats which will be rolled in bundles of 8.   These

(2)

These with Officers surplus kits will be dumped on "Hdqrs" and Coy's Dumps near Orderly Room by 6-0 p.m. and left in charge of Coy. Q.M.Sgts. The Transport Officer will arrange for their removal to Q.M. dump on empty ration limbers.

8. Special attention is drawn to the refills for Tommies Cookers which are being issued today, these must not be used until the Companies arrive in the front line.
There are provisions in RAILWAY WOOD for supplying hot water for tea by means of braziers.

9. The Transport Officer will arrange for 10. Pack Mules to report at present Battalion Hdqrs. at 7-30 p.m. for Transport of Lewis Guns and Hdqrs. kit,
No wheeled transport will be required for this move.

10. All Companies will render a trench strength return to the Adjutant by ~~8~~ 11 am. shewing numbers of Officers and O.Rs. actually proceeding into the line and giving details of location of the remaining Officers and men of their Coy's.

11. ACKNOWLEDGE.

Captain & Adjutant.
1/5th. East Lancs Regt.

Issued by orderly at .....11..... A.M.

Copy No. 1. "A" Coy.
"   "   2 "B" "
"   "   3 "C" "
"   "   4 "D" "
"   "   5 Commanding Officer.
"   "   6 Signalling Officer.
"   "   7 Int, Officer.
"   "   8 Q.M.
"   "   9 T.O.
"   " 10 War Diary.
"   " 11   "   "
"   " 12 File.

SECRET   Copy No 9
     1/5th Bn East Lancs Regt Order No 31.
                                         Sept 7th 17

Ref Maps
1/10.000 { ZONNEBEKE
         { ZILLEBEKE
1/20.000   28 N.W.

3

1. The Battn will relieve the 1/10th Manchester Regt to-night the 7th/8th in the front line
   (a) "B" Coy will relieve "B" Coy 1/10th Manch Regt in the right front line.
   (b) "D" Coy will relieve "A" Coy 1/10th Manch Regt in the Left front line.
   (c) "C" Coy will relieve "C" Coy 1/10th Manch Regt in support at I.6.d.8.7.
   (d) "A" Coy will relieve "D" Coy 1/10th Bn Manch Regt in reserve at LAKE FARM.

2. "A" & "C" Coys will proceed from Camp at YPRES SOUTH at 7-0 pm, via :-
   KROISSITAT - WARRINGTON ROAD (CORDUROY ROAD South of YPRES) - GORDON HOUSE to BIRR Cross Roads where 2 guides for each Coy, from the 1/10th Bn Manch Regt will meet them at 8·45 pm.

3. "B" Coy will clear RAILWAY WOOD, DUG OUT by 9 pm, and "D" Coy by 9-30 pm.
   4 guides per Coy will report to the

Coys Hdqrs of these Coys from "B" & "A" Coys
1/10th Manch Regt, respectively at 8-45 pm
They will be distributed as under:—

"B" Company

1st guide	LEFT POST	27. OR. & 1. L.G.
2nd guide	CENTRE "	1 Off & 54. ORks
		2 L.G. & Coy Hdqrs.
3rd "	RIGHT "	23. ORks.
4th "	SUPPORT	1 Off, 49. ORks, 1 L.G.

"D" Company

1st guide	No. 1. POST	7. ORks.
2nd "	2 "	22. ORks & 1. L.G.
3rd "	3 "	4. ORks & M.G. Post
" "	4 "	8. ORks & L.G.
" "	5 "	11. ORks & L.G.
" "	6 "	23. ORks & L.G.
" "	7 "	Advd Hdqrs
" "	8 "	7. ORks.
4th "	9 "	29. ORks & Coy Hdqr.

(NOTE: All numbers are approximate, Coy will
therefor equalize proportionately
according to the Strengths of their Coys)

4. The Int Officer will arrange for two
guides to the BIRR CROSS ROADS at
10-10 pm to meet Hdqrs and 2 Coys
of the 1/9th Manchester Regt and
conduct them to RAILWAY WOOD
DUG-OUT.

These guides to report to the Adjutant on completion of duty.

5. Dress for relieving troops will be as laid down in 1/5 th Bn East Lancs Regt Order No 30. para 3. with the following amendments 6 petrol tins per platoon & 2 petrol tins per Coy Hdqrs, will be carried full. No further issue will be made in the line "B" & "D" Coys will carry 25 Shovels each, to be drawn from Bde Dumps.

6. Lewis Guns and Magazines as laid down in 1/5 th Bn East Lancs Regt, Order No 30 para 4.
   (a) For "A" & "C" Coys in the same manner as in the above order.
   (b) For "B" & "D" Coys, man handled.

7. Paras (6) & (7) 1/5 Bn East Lancs Regt Order No 30 will stand for this relief in the case of "A" & "C" Coys

8. Rations for Hdqrs, "B" & "D" Coys for the 8th inst will be sent to BIRR Cross Roads by 6-30pm also one Water Cart.
Carrying parties will be sent by Coys and all petrol tins filled.
The Transport Officer will arrange for the carriage of "A" & "C" Coys petrol tins on Pack Mules up to the same point as the Lewis Guns.

The Quartermaster in conjunction with the Transport Officer will arrange for the removal of all stores, cookers, tools & water carts from the camp at YPRES-SOUTH, to the Dump as soon as 'A' Coy & 'C' Coys have vacated it.
The necessary certificate re-cleanliness being rendered to the Area Commandant by the Assistant Adjutant from Rear Hqrs.

9. The Regtl Aid Post will be situated in the Railway Embankment I 6. d 8 9. (near Support Coy.)
Medical Personnel will proceed with 'C' Coy from BIRR CROSS ROADS at 8·45 pm.

10 Battn Hqrs will be situated at KIT & KAT and will consist of 4 Officers (C.O. Adjt, Sigs Off & Int Off.) and 18 O.R.Ks viz:-

Signallers	5
Runners	8
Scout Sgt	1
Clerk	1
Batmen	3

All surplus to the above will be attached to "C" Coy. Arrangements being made by Sig Officer & Int Off for them to join 'C' Coy at BIRR. CROSS ROADS at 8·45 pm.

11 Completions of relief will be reported to Battn Hqrs, KIT & KAT by the following

means.
"B" & "D" Coys by runners (only means of communication)
C. Coy by wire.
A. Coy by wire through Bde Forward Station LAKE FARM, where a runner will be continually on duty to receive messages.

12. All trench stores will be taken over and receipts obtained.
These will be forwarded to Batt. Hdqrs as soon as possible after completion of relief, and before 4 am on the 8th inst.

13. Acknowledge

    [signature] Capt & Adjt
    1/5th Bn East Lancs Regt

Issued/Orders at 2 am
Copy No	1	OC "A" Coy
✓	2	B
✓	3	C
✓	4	D
✓	5	1/10th Manchester Regt
✓	6	Sig Off, Int Off, M.O.
✓	7	Q.M., T.O.
✓	8	Rear Hdqrs
✓	9	War diary
✓	10	do
✓	11	File
	12	

SECRET 4 Copy No. 8

1/5th Bn East Lancs Regt Order No 32

Ref Maps) 1/10000
FREZENBERG   Aug 8th 17

1. The Battn will occupy SANS SOUCI FARM tonight and establish a permanent post there of 1 Officer & 20 men.
   As it is possible that this position is held only weakly by the enemy by day an attempt will be made by a fighting patrol to occupy the post at dusk (8.45pm) tonight.

2. This patrol which will consist of not less than 20 men of No 13 Platoon "D" Coy will be under the command of 2/Lt S D. COOKE.

3. 3 Battalion Scouts are attached to the above platoon and can be used for any preliminary reconnoitering.

4. If this attempt is successful, the post will be immediately consolidated and made defensible against counter-attack.

5. Upon receipt of information of success of this patrol, OC "D" Coy will at once send any further reinforcements or tools that may be required.

6. If fighting patrol is unable to occupy the position, they will withdraw to their front line posts

7. In the event of such withdrawal an attack will be made by two

platoons of 'D' Coy with the object of capturing the position and destroying its occupants.

Platoons will attack simultaneously from either flank.

Zero for this attack will be 4 am, on the morning of the 9th inst (tomorrow).

8. There will be no Artillery barrage, and the patrol or the subsequent attack must endeavour to take full advantage of the element of surprise and carry out their task with rifle & bayonet.

9. Upon sounds of fighting and rifle fire coming from this position, 126 Machine Gun Coy will from a position in rear sweep with bursts of searching fire the paths leading from ZONNEBEKE, REDOUBT to the HANNEBEEK STREAM, the banks of that stream and the ground in front of SANS SOUCI, East of a line drawn N and S through J.2.a. central.

10. OC 'B' Coy will give all possible assistance with fire from No 3 POST and the Lewis Gun therein, and should pay particular attention to any enemy parties attempting to cross or ford the stream.

11. In the event of it being necessary for the attack by the two platoons to be carried out by 'D' Coy the Front line posts held by them would be left very weakly garrisoned. To meet this the two platoons

of 'C' Coy, which will tonight be digging the new trench about 150 yds N.E. of SEXTON-HOUSE, will be told off under arrangements between OC 'C' Coy & OC 'D' Coy with suitable parties for the various posts, and OC 'D' Coy will arrange that such parties relieve his garrison that are weakened or withdrawn. For tactical purposes, these two platoons of 'C' Coy will come under the command of OC 'D' Coy from 8.45 pm this evening and will if placed in front line posts hold them at all costs.

12. Should a withdrawal from SANS SOUCI be necessary in the case of the two platoon attack, the troops concerned will if darkness permits of the movements withdraw to the WEST of WESTHOEK RIDGE and will there reorganize and occupy the support trenches at I.6.a.8.7. otherwise they will occupy shell hole positions between existing posts.

13. Separate instructions have been issued to OC 'B' Coy with reference to action of his patrols on right battalion front tonight.

14. Remaining position of support Coy (C) and reserve Coy (A) will remain throughout the night in readiness to move at a moments notice on receipt of orders from the Battalion Commander.

15. Communication will be by runners throughout forward of Battn Hdqrs.

16. In the event of the S O S being sent up from SANS SOUCI or front line post Artillery barrage will come down on a line from I.2 b 10.05 through I.2 a 85.60 — D 26 c. 71.16 to D.26 c 35.50.

17. Dress for two platoon attack will be fighting dress, water bottles full, one days ration, and Iron rations in pack.
Each Bomber to carry 6 Bombs and rifle grenadiers to carry 6 grenades.
S.O.S. Grenades will be carried by Officers
OC "D" Coy will arrange necessary proportion of tools.

                                       E.J.Nolte
                                       Capt & Adjt

Issued to representatives
at 6.40 pm.   15th Bn Eastern Ontario Regt

Copy No 1   OC D Coy
       2   "   C   "
       3   "   B   "
       4   "   A   "
       5   Lieut Kelly 12b M G Coy   } Issued by
       6   126th Infy Bde   } orderly at
       7   War Diary   } 8 p
       8   — do —
       9   File
     10   Spare

SECRET   5   Copy No 11
1/5th Bn East Lancs Regt. Order No 23

Ref Maps
1/20,000 Sheets   Sept 10th 17
28 N.W and N.E.

1. The Battalion will be relieved in the
front line by the 1/9th Bn Manchester Regt
on the night of 10th/11th inst
R.F. B Coy is relieved by D Coy 9th Manchr
   L.F. D   "   "   A   "
   Support C   "   "   A   "
   Reserve A   "   "   B   "

2. On relief Coys will proceed
independently to camping ground at
YPRES SOUTH AREA via BIRR CROSS ROADS
GORDON HOUSE — WARRINGTON ROAD —
KRUISSTRAAT.
Distances of 100 yds will be left between
half platoons.

3. Guides for relieving battalion will be found
as follows:—
(a) B Coy will provide 4 guides to be at
~~BIRR CROSS ROADS~~ RAILWAY WOOD DUGOUT at 7.30p at 9 pm to report
to O.C D Coy 9th Manchester Regt.
(b) Hdqrs will provide 4 guides to be at
~~BIRR CROSS ROADS~~ RAILWAY WOOD DUGOUT at 7.30p at 9 pm to report
to O.C A 9th Manchester Regt, these
guides will bring the Coy forward
to Batt. Hdqrs.

where guides to be provided by O.C. "D" Coy will meet them, and take them forward. The latter guides to report at Battn Hdqrs at 10.30 p.m.

(c) "C" Coy will provide four guides to report to OC "C" Coy @ BIRR CROSS ROADS DUG-OUT at 7.15 pm.

(d) "A" Coy will provide four guides to report to OC "B" Coy @ Manchester Post at RAILWAY WOOD. DUG.OUT at 7.30 pm.

All guides must be given written instructions showing who they have to report to, time and post for which they are to guide.

Numbering of front line posts must be strictly in accordance with sketch map issued by 126th Inf Bde, that is right to left.

   Nos 1-3 posts Right Coy.
   SANS SOUCI & No 4-10 posts, Left Coy.

4. Patrolling on the night of relief is to be carried out by the outgoing companies, patrol reports being handed in to incoming Coy Hdqrs and patrols to rejoin the Battn independently.

5. All trench stores will be handed over and receipts obtained. Lists of Stores to be forwarded to Battn Hdqrs by noon on the 11th inst.

all petrol tins brought in and not actually taken over from previous Unit as trench stores will be brought out.
No entrenching tools (i.e, shovels & picks) will be brought out.

6. The Transport Officer will arrange for pack transport for Lewis Guns and magazines, according to the time table given below to be at the point on the Corduroy Road about I.17.a.85.90. where mules were unloaded when moving up to the line.

12 midnight	4 Pack animals	"	'A' Coy
1 am.	3	"	"	C Coy (less 1 gun)
1.30 am	5	"	"	D " (plus 1 gun)
do	4	"	"	B Coy
do	2	"	"	H.Qrs Coy.

Should Coys arrive at the above mentioned point before the time stated for their pack animals, Guns & magazines will be dumped and two men per section left with them to load.
All petrol tins will be dumped at the same place, and one man per platoon and one NCO per Coy will remain behind to load them on to two limbers which will be detailed by the Transport Officer to be there by 1-30 am.

7. 2/Lieut H.G Lancaster will take over the camp site at YPRES SOUTH vacated by

the 1/9th Battn Manchester Rgt. and allott canvas and bivouacs to Coy QM Sgt.

All arrangements as regards rations cookers, watercarts, haversacks, greatcoats and Officers Kits, will be carried out by him in conjunction with the Transport Officer and Quartermaster.

Guides to meet Coys should be sent to the point where the Corduroy Road enters the main road at KRUISSTRAAT at 2 am.

8. Completion of relief will be reported to Battn HQrs, KOT & KNT and Coys will report all present or otherwise on arrival at new Camp.

9. ACKNOWLEDGE

                       Capt & Adjt
                15th The East Lancs Regt.

Issued by Orderly at 11.30 pm
Copy No 1 OC A Cy
    "   2   " B "
    "   3   " C "
    "   4   " D "   Copy No 10 War Diary
    "   5   1/9th Manch Rgt   11 File
    "   6   Sig Off & M.O.
    "   7   T.O. & Q.M.
    "   8   Lieut R Lancaster
    "   9   War Diary

S E C R E T.   Copy No 1.

1/5th, Bn East Lancs Regt. Order No 34.

Ref, Map Sheet 28.N.W. & N.E.   13th, September 1917.

1. (a) 1/4th, Bn, East Lancs Regt, has been ordered to relieve the 1/9th, Bn, Manchester Regt, in the front line on the night of the 13/14th September 1917.

    (b) The Battalion will replace the 1/4th, Bn, East Lancs Regt, in Brigade Support with distribution as follows :-
    "Hqrs"? "A" & "C" Coy's in RAILWAY WOOD, DUGOUT.
    2 Platoons "B" Coy in LAKE FARM.
    1 Platoon "B" Coy, in O.B. 1 near RAILWAY WOOD.
    "B" Coy less 3 Platoons, in YPRES SOUTH.
    "D" "   in YPRES XXXXX.

2. "Hdqrs", 3 Platoons "B" Coy, "A" Coy, and "C" Coy will proceed in the above order from present camp at 8-0 p.m. by KRUISSTRAT, WARRINGTON ROAD (CORDUROY ROAD, South of YPRES) GORDON HOUSE to vicinity of BIRR CROSS ROADS.
Head of Column to reach BIRR CROSS ROADS 10-10 p.m. where guides will meet.
O.C. "D" Coy will arrange his own details for relief of "A" Coy, of the 1/4th Bn, East Lancs Regt, at the CLOTH HALL YPRES.

3. Dress for marching out.:-
Fighting dress, less greatcoats, flares, bombs, rifle grenades and entrenching tools (i.e. picks and shovels.)
The following will be carried in the pack.:-
Groundsheets, cardigan, one pair of socks, two days rations plus the emergency ration.
170, Rounds of S.A.A. per man will be carried.
6.Petrol Tins per Platoon and 2 Petrol Tins per Coy, Hdqrs will be carried full for use in RAILWAY WOOD & LAKE FARM.

4. 4 Lewis Guns per Coy, and 24 magazines per gun will be taken forward on Limbers, one limber to each Coy, these will proceed at 4-0 p.m. this afternoon under an N.C.O. & one man from each Coy, they will then be dumped in daylight, just off the Corduroy track, where mules were unloaded before, about I,17.a.85.90.
They will then be got ready for immediate issue as the troops march past.
Petrol Tins will be carried also on these limbers.

5. 1 Officer to be detailed by O.C. "C" Coy with 1 Platoon of "C" Coy & 5 N.C.O's "A" Coy, will proceed with the above limbers at 4-0 pm and will take over accomodation and duties in RAILWAY DUGOUT, he will report to the Adjutant 1/4th, Bn, East Lancs Regt, on arrival. The R.S.M. will accompany this party, to detail the duties required and take over "Hqrs" accomodation.

6. Distance of 100 yards between half platoon will be maintained on leaving this camp for move forward, half platoons proceeding in file special attention must be paid to keeping touch between half platoons.

7. All surplus kit to that being carried on the man will be packed in haversacks except greatcoats which will be rolled in bundles of 8 (Eight). These with Officers surplus kit will be dumped on "Hdqrs" and Coy's dumps near Orderly Room by 6-0p.m. and left in charge of Coy, Q.M.Sgts, The Transport Officer will arrange for their removal to Q.M. dump on empty ration limbers.

SECRET   Copy No 7
1/5th Bn East Lancs Regt Order No 35.

Ref Map Sheets 28 N.W. & N.E.
                                         Sept 15th 17

1. On the night of the 15th/16th, the 1/4th Batn East Lancs Regt, has been ordered to take over a portion of the front held by the 125th Inf Bde, from the YPRES-RULERS RAILWAY exclusive to the ROAD which runs from D 26 a 3.0 to D 25. d 40.45. inclusive.
The inter Brigade Boundary will then run from D 25 d 40.45. to the Centre of WYLD WOOD at I 6. b 6 2 and thence to GULLY FARM.

2. Troops of the 1/4th Batn East Lancs Regt used to carry out this operation will be replaced by the Battalion as under.
'C' Coy less one Platoon to I 6. b 8.9.
one platoon 'C' Coy to LAKE FARM.
'D' Coy replace 'C' Coy in RAILWAY WOOD DUGOUT.

3. 'D' Coy will proceed by march route from YPRES at 6-30pm, via:- MENIN-GATE, HELL FIRE CORNER, and thence by track to RAILWAY WOOD.
Four NCO's 'D' Coy will proceed at once on receipt of these orders to RAILWAY WOOD

Issued by Orderly at 3 pm

Copy No 1   OC 'A' Coy
       2   'B'
       3   'C'
       4   'D'
       5   Rear Hdqrs
       6   Sig Off & MO
       7   War Diary
       8   do
       9   File

to take over accommodation in the DUGOUT from "C" Coy.

4. "C" Coy will clear RAILWAY WOOD DUGOUT by 8 pm and will proceed independantly to their new post. No guides will be provided for 1.6.c.8.9., but two Battalion Scouts will report to OC "C" Coy by 7-45 pm as guides for LAKE FARM.

5. OC "D" Coy will make necessary arrangements for Transport, direct with the Transport Officer.

6. Two days Rations & Water will be carried by all troops concerned in these moves.

7. "C" Coy on completion of their relief will come under the command of the OC 1/4th Batn East Lancs Regt.

8. All Trench Stores, Ammunition etc, will be taken over and receipts given. Copies of these receipts to be sent to Batn Hdqrs by 9 am on the 16th.

9. Completion of reliefs will be wired to Batn Hdqrs which will remain in RAILWAY WOOD. "C" Coy to report their message to 1/4th Bn East Lancs Regt. (N.T.B. Station Call)

10. Acknowledge by wire

Capt & Adjt
1/5th Bn East Lancs Regt

Addendum No 1 to   Copy No 10

1/5th Bn East Lancs Regt Order No 26

Sept 16th 17

1. Ref Para 4
      Dinner for guides will be put back 2 hours.
2. Para 5   For "7-30 pm" read "9-30 pm"
3. Para 6   For "9-30 pm" read "11-0 pm"
4. Train Time Table Para 3.
      A Train will leave the YPRES ASYLUM SIDING at 3.30 am on the 17th inst. Accommodation allotted for 480 all ranks of this Unit.
   The allotment of carriages is 4 Officers or 8 O.Rks. to a compartment.
   The Battalion will detrain at the second stopping place ie. level crossing G.11.a.9.9.

   Rear Hdqrs will arrange guides to be at level crossing G.11.a.9.9. at 3.30 am. to meet Coys on detraining.
   No Baggage of any kind is allowed on this Train.
5. Hot Meals.
      The Quartermaster will arrange for two cookers to be at suitable site within vicinity of Siding at YPRES

ASYLUM by midnight, these cookers will
supply tea to the boys on arrival at
this point
Care must be taken not to block the main
road while issuing the tea.
6. Extra Guides
OC "C" Coy will arrange for
1 Platoon "C" Coy at T.6.d.89 to provide two
guides to report to the Adjutant at
RAILWAY WOOD DUGOUT at 10 pm to guide
two platoons of the 12th Batt Royal
Scots to the embankment T.6.d.89.
The 1 Platoon "C" Coy will however
withdraw as per previous orders, only
two hours later, that is 10 pm.
7. ACKNOWLEDGE.

Capt & Adjt
15th Bn East Lancs Regt

Issued to all recipients of
15th East Lancs Regt Order No 36
by Orderly at 4.30 pm.

SECRET   Copy No 10

1/5th Bn. East Lancs Regt. Order No 36

Ref Maps Sheets 28 N.W. & N.E.   Sept 16/17

1. The Battalion will be relieved by the 13th Bn (S) ROYAL SCOTS, less one Company on the night 16th/17th inst in accordance with Table under Para 2.

2. Hdqrs, 'A' Coy, 'D' Coy, & 'B' Coy less two platoons will be relieved at RAILWAY WOOD by Hdqrs, 'A' & 'D' Coys of the Royal Scots.
'C' Coy less one platoon and 2 platoons 'B' Coy at LAKE FARM, will be relieved by 'B' Coy of the Royal Scots.
One Platoon 'C' Coy at I.6.d.89. will withdraw independantly at 8pm.

3. On relief, companies will proceed independantly to the ASYLUM, YPRES, from which point, they will train to BRANDHOEK, No1 and be located at RIDGE CAMP G.11.a.45.
Train time table will be notified later.

4. Guides for the incoming unit will be found as under:—
2 Guides (Bn Scouts) to report at RED ROSE CAMP. H.1.b.80. at 2.30 pm for advance party to take over.

duties and dugout accommodation at RAILWAY WOOD.

4 Guides (Bn Scouts) to report at the ASYLUM SIDING YPRES at 6pm to guide Hdqrs, 'A', 'B' & 'D' Coys of the relieving unit to BIRR CROSS ROADS. These guides will ensure that the Party proceed in the following order, Hdqrs, "A" Coy, D Coy, and "B" Coy.

5 guides each from 'A' & 'D' Coys will report at BIRR CROSS ROADS at 7-15 pm to guide like Coys of the relieving battalion to RAILWAY WOOD Dugout.

5 Guides from LAKE FARM will report at BIRR CROSS ROADS at 7-30 pm to guide 'B' Coy of the relieving battalion to LAKE FARM.

5. 'A' & 'D' Coys must clear RAILWAY Dugout by 7-30 pm, but will not move back until relieving Coys actually arrive.

6. One Limber per Coy for Lewis Guns and magazines will be at the point where the light railway crosses the Corduroy road about I.17.a.56. at 9-30 pm. Coys passing this point before the above time hour will dump their L.Gs. and magazines and leave them in charge of an NCO & one man

who will load same immediately on arrival of the Transport.

All petrol tins brought into the line will be taken out, and sent down on those Limbers.

The Limbers will proceed direct to RIDGE CAMP.

2. All trench Maps (paper) Aeroplane photograph Sketches, trench and area stores will be handed over to relieving Unit and receipts obtained, to be forwarded to Battn Hdqrs, immediately on arrival at new Camp. All trench Stores must be collected into Coy Dumps and every effort made, to salve as many of the stores scattered about about the area as possible, even though they may not have been handed over to Coys.

3. Care must be taken that all vacated trenches dugouts and camps are left thoroughly clean. Usual certificates of cleanliness will be obtained from the relieving Coys by Coy Commanders and from the Area Commandant by the Quarter-master for the Dumps area.

These will be forwarded to Battn Hdqrs at RIDGE CAMP by 9 am on the 19th inst

9. Baggage Wagons will be sent to the camps tomorrow at times to be arranged between Rear HdQrs and OC 143rd Coy ASC.

No motor transport is available for the move, and if necessary first line transport and baggage wagons must do two journeys to the new Area.

10. Batt. establishment of S.A.A, Grenades &c will be carried on wheels.

11. Special arrangements have already been made for the Camps allotted to be taken over by a party from the details under the orders of MAJOR KERR D.S.O, M.C., who is supervising camps and areas for the Brigade.

Rear HdQrs will get into communication with the above Officer as soon as possible and ensure that all necessary arrangements are being made.

12. All transports will march under the Brigade Transport Officer starting at 5.30pm.

The new Brigade Transport Lines are situated at YORK CAMP a.5.d.04.

13. Guides for the Battalion on arrival at BRANDHOEK Not will be detailed by Rear HdQrs to suit time table of trains, when issued, hot meals also will be

arranged accordingly.

14. 100 yds between half platoons will be maintained for march to YPRES, and in day marching WEST of YPRES to BRANDHOEK there will be 200 yds maintained between platoons.

15. Completion of relief will be reported to Batn HdQrs RAILWAY WOOD. After all companies have completed, Battn HQrs will move to RIDGE CAMP.

16. ACKNOWLEDGE by wire.

[signature]
Capt Adjt

Issued by Runner
at 5 am

Copy No	1	O C "A" Coy
	2	" B "
	3	" C "
	4	" D "
	5	REAR HQ
	6	MAJOR KERR, DSO, MC
	7	O/C (S) Bn Royal Scots
	8	Sig Off & M O
	9	War Diary
	10	do
	11	File

SECRET.   Copy No. 11

1/5th Bn, East Lancs Regt, Order No 37.

War Diary 9

18th, September 1917.

Ref, Maps Sheet 28N.W. & 27.N.E. 1/20,000.

1. 126th, Infy, Bde, Group has been ordered to move from the BRANDHOEK AREA to WINNEZEELE AREA No,1 on the 19th, inst,. Route via SWITCH ROAD, North of POPERINGHE, Road Junction L.4.b.8.2. WATOU and EROGLANDT.

2. The head of Battalion will pass the starting point at 5-40 a.m., order of march will be "Hdqrs", "B", "C", "D" and "A" Coy,. The starting point will be Cross Roads J.5.c.92.

3. Distances of 300 yds, between Companies will be maintained EAST of POPERINGHE, Coy's will close up AT the first hourly halt after passing the Cross Roads L.4.b.82. This halt will be FOR 20 minutes to enable this to be carried out. After this point the Battalion will march closed up.

4. Halts from 10 minutes to the clock hour to the clock hour and from 5 minutes to the half hour to the half hour will be observed throughout the march except the 20 minutes halt mentioned in Para 3.

5. All Transport of the Brigade Group will march under the Brigade Transport Officer, 1st, Line Transport of the Battalion will pass the starting point at 8-16 a.m. A gap of 200 yds will be left between the Transport of units and a gap of 20 yds between each group of 6 vehicles. Transport will not observe the hour and half hourly halts until the halt at 9-50 a.m.

6. 2/Lieut R.G. FARNELL and one N.C.O. to be detailed by O.C "A" Coy will be detailed to march in rear of the Brigade Column to collect all men of the Battalion who are given leave to fall out by an Officer but who are not admitted by a Medical Officer to an Ambulance Wagon. These men will be marshalled into a formed body by the above Officer and marched as such to their destination.

7. The Signalling Officer will obtain Brigade time before 9-0 pm. tonight and synchronize the watches of all Officers before 10-0 p.m.

8. ACKNOWLEDGE.

Issued by Orderly at....P.M.

Captain & Adjutant
1/5th, Bn, East Lancs Regt.

```
Copy No. 1.  "A" Coy.
  "    "  2   "B"   "
  "    "  3   "C"   "
  "    "  4   "D"   "
  "    "  5   2nd in Command.
  "    "  6   Q.M.
  "    "  7   T.O.
  "    "  8   Sig Off.
  "    "  9   M.O.
  "    " 10   War Diary
  "    " 11     "    "
  "    " 12   File.
```

Received one Copy of 1/5th, Bn East Lancs Regt Order No 37 d/ 18-9-17.

SECRET.   Copy. No. 7

10

1/5th. Bn. East Lancs Regt, Order No. 58.
                                                              20/9/17.

Ref, Maps Sheet 27, 1/40,000.

1. The Battalion will move by march route on September 21st, 19th 1917. to the WORMHOUDT AREA.

2. The starting point for the Battalion will be the junction of lane from Battalion Headquarters and Main Road WATOU-WINNEZEELE. (J.12.c.19.)

3. Coy's will march in the following order:- "C" Coy, "A" Coy, HQrs, "B" Coy & "D" Coy. "C" Coy will pass the starting point at 10-0 a.m.

4. 1st. Line Transport will proceed under Brigade Arrangements and will pass the Brigade Starting Point J.16.b.26. at 9-11. a.m.

5. Officers Baggage and Mess stores will be sent to the Q.M. Stores by 8-0 a.m. and will be loaded by a party of 1 N.C.O. and 12 men to be detailed by "O.C" "C" Coy which will proceed with the Transport as baggage guard.

6. Acknowledge.

                                              [signature]
                                              Captain & Adjutant
                                              1/5th. Bn. East Lancs Regt.

Issued by orderly at 10 P.M.

Copy No 1 "A" Coy.
  "   " 2 "B" "
  "   " 3 "C" "
  "   " 4 "D" "
  "   " 5 Q.M. & T.O.
  "   " 6 Sig Off & M.O.
  "   " 7 War Diary.
  "   " 8 "   "
  "   " 9 File.

SECRET.   Copy No. 8

            1/5th. Bn, East Lancs Regt, Order No. 39.

Map Ref. Sheet 19 & 27. 1/40,000.   21st September 1917.

1. The Battalion will move to TETECHEN tomorrow the 22nd. inst,
   by March Route.

2. Coy's will parade for marching out on Coy's Parades at 8-50 a.m.
   Order of March will be as follows.:- "A" Coy, "D" Coy, "Hdqrs"
   Coy, "B" Coy, and "C" Coy,
   The Band will follow "D" Coy.

3. 1st Line Transport will march in rear of the Battalion and
   and closed up and will join the column at the starting point
   C.11.b.67. except for Cookers, Water Carts, Maltese, Mess Cart
   and Baggage Wagons which will follow the Battalion from the
   present billeting area and join their correct position with the
   remainder of the 1st. Line Transport at the starting point.

4. The usual hourly halts will be observed. In addition there will
   be a halt of one and a half hours from 12 noon to 1-30 p.m.
   for the mid-day meal.
   "O.C" Coy's will ensure that Cookers are not brought up from
   the rear in such a way as to block the roads.
   Horses will be fed and watered, the patrol tins carried on the
   limbers being employed for this purpose.

5. Steel Helmets will be worn on the march.

6. Officers baggage and mess stores will be dumped at the
   Q.M. Stores by 7-30 am prompt and will be loaded on the baggage
   wagons by an N.C.O. and 12 men to be detailed by O.C. "B" Coy.
   1 Motor Lorry will be available for the moving of surplus stores.
   this lorry will do two journeys to the new area.

7. The Signalling Officer will arrange to place one cyclist orderly
   at the disposal of Major KERR, D.S.O.,M.C. Who is marshalling
   the transport at the starting point.
   He will also arrange for correct Brigade Time being obtainable
   from the orderly room at 8-0 am.

8. ACKNOWLEDGE.

                                            Captain & Adjutant
                                          1/5th. Bn, East Lancs Regt.

Issued by Orderly at 12. midnight.

Copy No. 1 "A" Coy.
     " 2 "B" "
     " 3 "C" "
     " 4 "D" "
     " 5 Q.M. and T.O.
     " 6 Sig Off and M.O.
     " 7 War Diary.
     " 8 "   "
     " 9 File.

SECRET.   Copy No. 8

1/5 Bn E. Lancs. Regt. Orders. No. 31.

Ref Maps.   Sept 7th 1917
1/10,000 Sheets { ZONNEBEKE
                { ZILLEBEKE
1/20,000 - 28 N.W.

1. The Battalion will relieve the
   1/10 Bn Manchester Regt tonight the
   7th/8th in the front line
   (a). 'B' Coy will relieve 'B' Coy 1/10 Manch Rgt in
        the right front line.
   (b). 'D' Coy will relieve 'A' Coy 1/10 Manch Rgt
        in the left front line.
   (c). 'C' Coy will relieve 'C' Coy 1/10 Manch
        in support at I 6.d.8.7.
   (d). 'A' Coy will relieve 'D' Coy 1/10 Manch Rgt
        in reserve at LAKE FARM.

2. 'A' & 'C' Coys will proceed from camp
   at YPRES SOUTH at 7.00pm via
   KRUSSITAT – WARRINGTON ROAD (CORDUROY
   ROAD South of YPRES) – GORDON HOUSE to
   BIRR Cross Roads where 2 guides
   for each company from the 1/10 Bn
   Manch Rgt will meet them at
   8.45 p.m.

3. 'B' Coy will clear RAILWAY WOOD DUG
   OUT by 9 pm and 'D' Coy by 9.30 pm
   4 Guides per Coy will report to the

Coy Hqrs of these Coys from 'B' & 'A' Coys
1/5. Manch Rgt respectively at 8.45 p.m.
They will be distributed as under:-

B Company.
1st Guide. Left POST.   27 OR. & 1 L.G.
2nd   "   Centre "   1 OH 54 OR.
                            2. L.G. & Coy HQ.
3rd   "   Right   "   XXXX 23 OR.
4:    "   Support   1 OH. 49 OR. 1. L.G.

D Company
1st Guide. No 1 POST.   7 OR.
2nd   "   No 2   "   22 OR & 1 L.G.
3rd   "   No 3   "   4 OR & M.G. Post.
 "   "   No 4   "   8 OR & L.G.
 "   "   No 5   "   11 OR & L.G.
 "   "   No 6   "   23 OR & L.G.
 "   "   No 7   "   Adv Hqrs.
 "   "   No 8   "   7 OR.
4:    "   No 9   "   29 OR & Coy HQ.

(Note:- All numbers are approximate,
Coys will therefore equalize
proportionately according to the strengths
of their Companies)

4. The Int Officer will arrange for
two guides to be BIRR CROSS ROADS
at 10.10 p.m. to meet Hqrs and 2
Coys of the 1/9. Bn Manchester Rgt
and conduct them to RAILWAY
WOOD DUGOUT.

these guides to report to the Adjutant on completion of duty.

5. Dress for relieving troops will be as laid down in 1/5: Bn E Lancs Lt Order No 30 Para.3 with the following amendments 6 petrol tins per platoon and 2 petrol tins per coy Hqrs will be carried full. No further issue will be made in the line 'B' & 'D' Coys will carry 25 shovels each, to be drawn from Bde Dump

6. Lewis Guns and magazines as laid in 1/5: Bn E Lancs Lt Order No 30 Para 4 will be taken forward
   (a) For 'A' & 'C' Coys in the same manner as in the above order ~~possibly~~
   (b) For 'B' & 'D' Coys man handled.

7. Paras (6) & (7) 1/5 Bn E Lancs Lt Order No 30 will stand for this relief in the case of 'A' & 'C' Coys.

8. Rations for Hqrs, 'B' & 'D' Coys for the 8th inst will be sent to BIRR Cross Roads by 6.30 pm also one water cart. Carrying parties will be sent by Coys and all petrol tins filled The Transport Officer will arrange for the carriage of 'A' & 'C' Coys petrols tins on pack mules up to the same point as the Lewis Guns. ~~this~~

8. The Quartermaster in conjunction with the Transport Officer will arrange for the removal of all stores, cookers, tools and water carts from the camp at YPRES SOUTH to the dump as soon as 'A' & 'C' Coys have vacated it. The necessary certificate re cleanliness being rendered to the Area Commandant by the Assistant Adjutant from Rear Hqrs.

9. The Regt Aid Post will be situated in the Railway Embankment I.6.d.89. (near Support Coy).
Medical Personnel will proceed with 'C' Coy from BIRR CROSS ROADS at 8.45p.

10. Bn Hqrs will be situated at KIT & KAT and will consist of 4 Officers (C.O; ADJ; Sigs; I.O.) and 18 OR.

   Signallers 5.
   Runners 8
   Scout Sgt 1
   Clerk 1
   Batmen 3.

All surplus to the above will be attached to 'C' Coy, arrangements being made by Sig. Officer and I.O. for them to join 'C' Coy at BIRR CROSS Roads at 8.45p.

11. Completion of relief will be reported to Bn Hqrs KIT & KAT by the following

means.
"B" & "D" Coys by runner (only means of communication)
"C" Coy by wire.
"A" " by wire through Bde Forward
　　　　Station. LAKE FARM where a
　　　　runner will be continually on
　　　　duty to receive messages.

12/ All trench stores will be taken
over and receipts obtained.
These will be forwarded to BnHqrs
as soon as possible after
completion of relief and before 4 a.m. on the 8th
inst.

13/ ACKNOWLEDGE.

　　　　　　　　　G.F.H. Bolton Capt & adj
　　　　　　　　　1/5 Bn E Lanc R

Issued by Orderly at 2.a.m.
　Copy No 1. "A" Coy
　"　No 2. "B"
　"　No 3. "C"
　"　No 4. "D"
　"　No 5. 1st Manch Rgt.
　"　No 6. Sig Off. Int Off. M.O.
　"　No 7. Q.M. & T.O.
　"　No 8. Rear HQ.
　"　No 9. War Diary
　"　No 10.   "
　"　No 11. File.

baggage party to load at
the above hour.
Coys will arrange to have
breakfasts at 2-45 am before
marching out instead of
Gun fire at 3-30 am

[signature]
Capt & Adjt
1/5th Bn East Surrey Regt

22/9/17

SECRET.   LEA 16/24

   OC A Coy
   "   B   "
   "   C   "
   "   D   "
   Sig Off
   QM
   S.O.
   R.S.M.

Ref 1/5th Bn. East Lanc's Regt. Order No 39. issued tonight.

Para.1. The Battalion will proceed to ADINKERKE.

Para.2. Coys will form up at the starting point at 6-0 am and not 5-am as stated. Coy Guides will be sent to report to 2/Lieut Lancaster at 5-30 am.

Para.3. Distance of 100 yds will be left in rear of half Battn and Transport.

Para.4. Officers baggage and mess stores will be dumped at 5-am O.C. 'D' Coy will detail

SECRET   17 Copy No. 9
          1/5th Bn East Lancs Regt ~~No 33~~
Ref Maps) 1/10000
FREZENBERG   8th 17

1. The Battn will occupy SANS.SOUCI.FARM. tonight and establish a permanent post there of 1 Officer & 30 men.
   As it is possible that this position is held only weakly by the enemy by day an attempt will be made by a fighting patrol to occupy the post at dusk (9.45p) tonight.

2. This patrol which will consist of not less than 20 men of No 13 Platoon 'D' Coy will be under the command of 2/Lt S.D. COOKE.

3. 3 Battalion Scouts are attached to the above platoon and can be used for any preliminary reconnoitring.

4. If this attempt is successful, the post will be immediately consolidated and made defencable against counter-attack.

5. Upon receipt of information of success of this patrol, OC 'D' Coy will at once send any further reinforcements or tools that may be required.

6. If fighting patrol is unable to occupy the position, they will withdraw to their front line posts

7. In the event of such withdrawal an attack will be made by two

platoons of 'D' Coy with the object of capturing the position and destroying its occupants.

Platoons will attack simultaneously from either flank.

Zero for this attack will be 4 am, on the morning of the 9th inst (tomorrow).

8. There will be no Artillery barrage, and the patrol or the subsequent attack must endeavour to take full advantage of the element of surprise and carry out their task with rifle & bayonet.

9. Upon sounds of fighting and rifle fire coming from this position, 126 Machine Gun Coy will from a position in rear sweep with bursts of searching fire the paths leading from ZONNEBEKE REDOUBT to the HANNEBEEK STREAM, the banks of that stream and the ground in front of SANS SOUCI, East of a line drawn N and S through J.2.a central.

10. OC 'B' Coy will give all possible assistance with fire from No 3 Post and the Lewis Gun therein, and should pay particular attention to any enemy parties attempting to cross or ford the stream.

11. In the event of it being necessary for the attack by the two platoons to be carried out by D Coy, the front line posts held by them would be left very weakly garrisoned. To meet this the two platoons

of "C" Coy, which will tonight be digging the new Trench about 150 yds. N.E. of SEXTON-HOUSE, will be told off under arrangements between OC "C" Coy & OC "D" Coy with suitable parties for the various posts, and OC "D" Coy will arrange that such parties relieve his garrison that are weakened or withdrawn. For tactical purposes, these two platoons of "C" Coy will come under the command of OC "D" Coy from 8.45 pm this evening and will if placed in front line posts hold them at all costs.

12. Should a withdrawal from SANS SOUCI be necessary in the case of the two platoon attack, the troops concerned will if darkness permits of the movements withdraw to the WEST of WESTHOEK RIDGE and will there reorganize and occupy the support trenches at I.6.a.8.7. otherwise they will occupy shell hole positions behind existing posts.

13. Separate instructions have been issued to OC "B" Coy with reference to action of his patrols on right battalion front tonight.

14. Remaining portion of support Coy (C) and reserve Coy (A) will remain throughout the night in readiness to move at a moment's notice on receipt of orders from the Battalion Commander.

15. Communication will be by runners throughout forward of Battn Hdqrs.

16. In the event of the S O S being sent up from SANS SOUCI or front line post Artillery barrage will come down on a line from S.2.b.10.05. through S.2.a.85.60. — D.26.c.71.16. to D.26.c.35.50.

17. Dress for two platoon attack will be fighting dress, water bottles full, one days ration, and Iron rations in pock.
Each Bomber to carry 6 Bombs and rifle grenadiers to carry 6 grenades.
S.OS. Grenades will be carried by Officers
OC "D" Coy will arrange necessary proportion of tools.

                                                              G.H.Holt

sned ~~by~~ representating   Capt & Adjt
    at 6.40 pm.   1/5th Dn East Lancs Regt

Copy No 1   OC D Coy
      2   "   C   "
      3   "   B   "
      4   "   A   "   } Issued by
      5   Lieut Kelly 126 M. G Coy   } orderly at 8p
      6   126th Inf Bde
      7   War Diary
      8   — do —
      9   File
      ~~No~~ Spare

1/5th Bn E. Lanc. Rgt. Order N° 33

Copy N° 11
13

Ref. Maps.   Sept. 10th 1917
Reproductions
28 N.W. and N.E.

(1) The Battalion will be relieved in
    the Front line by the 1/7 Bn Manch Rgt.
    on the night of the 10/11th inst.
    R.F.   B Coy is relieved   by "D" Coy 9th Manch
    L.F.   D   "   "   " "A" & S.A.
    Supp. C   "   "   " "C" & S.A.
    Reserve A   "   "   " "B"   "

(2) On relief Coys will proceed
    independently to camping ground
    at YPRES SOUTH AREA via BIRR CROSS
    ROADS – GORDON HOUSE – WARRINGTON
    ROAD – KRUISSTRAAT.
    Distances of 100 yds will be left
    between half platoons.

(3) Guides for relieving Battalion will
    be found as follows:-

(a) "B" Coy will provide 4 guides to
    be at BIRR CROSS ROADS at 9 p.m.
    to report to O.C. D Coy. 9th Manch Rgt

(b) "HQ" will provide 4 guides to be at
    RAILWAY WOOD DUGOUT at 7.30 p.m.
    ~~BIRR CROSS ROADS at~~ 9 p.m. to report
    to O.C. A Coy 9th Manch Rgt, these guides
    will bring the Coy forward to Bn HQrs

whose guides to be provided by OC 'D' Coy
will meet them and take them forward.
The latter guides to report at Bn Hqrs
at 10.30 p.m.
(c) C Coy will provide four guides to
report to OC C Coy 9" Manch Regt at
BIRR CROSS ROADS at 9 p.m.
~~RAILWAY WOOD DUGOUT at 7.15 p.m.~~
(d) A Coy will provide four guides to
report to OC B Coy 9" Manch Regt at
RAILWAY WOOD DUGOUT at 7.30 p.m.
All guides must be given written
instructions showing who they have to
report to, time and post for which
they are a guide.
Numbering of front line posts must
be strictly in accordance with sketch
map issued by sub Sect Cdr that is
right to left
    No 1 - Right Coy
SANS SOUCI & NE 1-4 = Left "
(4) Patrolling on the night of relief is to
be carried out by the outgoing companies,
patrol reports being handed in to
incoming Coy Hqrs and patrols to
report to Bn independently.
(5) All trench stores will be handed over
and receipts obtained. Lists of stores
to be forwarded to Bn Hqrs by noon
on the 4th inst.

(a) All petrol tins brought in and not actually taken over from previous unit as trench stores will be brought out. No entrenching tools (shovels and picks) will be brought out.

(b) The Transport Officer will arrange for pack transport for Lewis Guns and Magazines etc according to the time table given below to be at the point on the Cambrai Road about I.17.a.85.90. where mules were unloaded when moving up to the line.

12 midnight	4 Pack Animals	"A" Coy
1. am.	3 " "	"C" " (less 1 gun)
1.30 am	5 " "	"D" " (plus 1 gun)
do.	4 " "	"B" "
do.	2 " "	"H.qrs" (1 for M.O.)

Should Coys arrive at the above mentioned point before the time stated for their pack animals, guns and magazines will be dumped and two men per section left with them to load.
All petrol tins will be dumped at the same place and one man per platoon and one NCO per Coy will remain behind to load them on to two limbers which will be detailed by the Transport Officer to be there by

1.30 a.m.

(7) 2/Lt. R.G. LANCASTER will take over the camp site at YPRES SOUTH vacated by the 1/9 Bn Manch Rgt. and allott canvas and bivouacs to Coy Q.M. Sgts. All arrangements in regards rations, cookers watercarts haversacks and greatcoats and officers Kits will be carried out by him in conjunction with the Transport Officer and Quartermaster.

(8) Guides to meet Coys should be sent to the point where the Corduroy Road enters the main road at KRUISSTAAT at 2 a.m.

(8) Completion of relief will be reported to Bn Hqrs. KIT KAT and Coys will report all present or otherwise on arrival at new camp.

(9) ACKNOWLEDGE

G.G.H. Bolton Capt + adj,
1/5th Bn E Lanc Rgt
Issued by orderly at 12.30 a.

Copy N°1. A Coy.   Copy N°7 T.O. + Q.M.
     N°2. B "   " 8 2/Lt LANCASTER
     N°3. C "   " 9 War Diary
     N°4. D "   " 10 " "
     N°5 1/9 Bn Manch Rgt.   " 11 File
     N°6 Sig. Off. MO   " " 12.

SECRET.   Copy No...7...

1/5th. Battn. East Lancs Regt. Order No. 40

Ref. Map.Sheet 19/1/40,000.   22nd September 1917.

1. The Battalion will move by march route tomorrow 23rd inst,
   to destination to be notified later.

2. The starting point for the Battalion will be Cross Roads,
   F.30.B.23. i.e. The Cross Roads about 800 yards on the
   DUNKERQUE Side of COUDEKERQUE AND on the COUDEKERQUE -
   DUNKERQUE Road.

3. Coy's will form up in the following order at the starting point
   at 5-0 a.m. "A" Coy, "C" Coy, "Hqrs Coy, "B" Coy, and "D" Coy.
   The band will follow "C" Coy.
   Coy Guides will be sent to report to 2/Lieut F.G. LANCASTER
   at the starting point at 4-45 a.m. to ascertain exact
   location and will return to guide their Coy's.

4. 1st Line Transport and Baggage Wagons will march in rear of
   the Battalion and closed up. "A" & "C" Coy's Cookers will
   join the Battalion at the starting point.

5. Officers baggage and mess stores will be dumped at the Q.M.
   Stores by 4-0 a.m. except "A" & "C" Coy's which will be collected by the Transport Officer at the same hour.
   "D" Coy will detail a loading party of 1 Sgt and 12 men to
   load baggage wagons at 4-0 am. and to act as baggage guard
   on the march.

6. Certificates of cleanliness of billets will be rendered with
   parade states at the starting point.

                                          Captain & Adjutant
                                          1/5th.Bn. East Lancs Regt.

Issued by orderly at..10.30..P.M.

Copy No. 1 "A" Coy.
  "   " 2 "B" "
  "   " 3 "C" "
  "   " 4 "D" "
  "   " 5 Sig Off, & M.O.
  "   " 6 Q.M. & T.O.
  "   " 7 War Diary
  "   " 8   "   "
  "   " 9 File.

13.

S E C R E T   Copy No. 7.

1/5th, Bn, East Lancs Regt, Order No. 41.

Ref. Map. 1/10,000. Sheet No.4.   24th.
                                                  BRAY, September 1917.

1. The Battalion will relieve the 2/5th, Bn East Lancashire Regt
   in the OOST DUNKERQUE BAINS SECTOR of the Coast Defences.

2. The Battalion will proceed by march route via COXYDE and
   COXYDE BAINS. Coy's will march in the following order :-
   "C" Coy, "A" Coy, "D" Coy, "B" Coy and "Hdqrs. Coy.
   "C" Coy. will enter the main road at 7.30 a.m.

3. Coy's will march closed up with intervals of 200 yards
   between Companies and there will be the same interval between
   columns of transport of the same length.

4. Steel helmets will be worn and box respirators at the alert
   position.

5. "O.C" "B" Coy. will detail his rear Platoon to act
   as rear party under the orders of 2/Lieut. P.G. LANCASTER.

6. All defence schemes, trench stores, maps etc, will be taken
   over and receipts given.

7. Officers Baggage & Mess stores will be dumped out side
   Battn. Hdqrs. Hut, by 7-30 a.m. prompt.
   One Officers servant per Coy. will be left with these stores.
   Loading will be done by rear party.

8. Usual certificates with regard to cleanliness of billets
   will be rendered by O.C. Coy's with parade states.

9. Battn Hdqrs will be situated at R. 27.d.0.6. on completion
   of move and transport lines at R.32.a.6.7.

                                          [signature]
                                          Captain & Adjutant.
                                          1/5th, Bn, East Lancs Regt.

Issued by Orderly at 6-30 am.
Copy No.1. O. C. "A" Coy
  "   2   "   "   "B" "
  "   3   "   "   "C" "
  "   4   "   "   "D" "
  "   5   Sig Off. & M.O.
  "   6   T.O. & Q.M.
  "   7   War Diary.
  "   8   "   "
  "   9   File.
  " 10   Spare.

SECRET.   File   Copy No. 11.

                           14

1/5th. Bn. East Lancs Regt. Order No. 34.

Ref. Map Sheet 28.N.W. & N.E.   13th. September 1917.

1. (a) 1/4th. Bn. East Lancs Regt. has been ordered to relieve the
       1/9th. Bn. MANCHESTER Regt. in the Front Line on the night
       of the 13/14th. September 1917.

   (b) The Battalion will replace the 1/4th. Bn. East Lancs Regt.
       in Brigade Support with distribution as follows :-
       "Hdqrs", "A" & "C" Coy's in RAILWAY WOOD DUGOUT.
       2 Platoons "B" Coy in LAKE FARM.
       1 Platoon "B" Coy, in O.B.1. near RAILWAY WOOD.
       "B" Coy less 3 Platoons in YPRES SOUTH.
       "D" Coy in YPRES.

2. "Hdqrs", 3 Platoons "B" Coy, "A" Coy, and "C" Coy, will proceed
   in the above order from present camp at 8-0 p.m. by KRUISSTRAT,
   WARRINGTON ROAD (CORDUROY ROAD, South of YPRES) GORDON HOUSE
   to vicinity of BIRR CROSS ROADS.
   Head of column to reach BIRR CROSS ROADS 10-10 p.m. where guides
   will meet.
   "O.C" "D" Coy, will arrange his own details for relief of "A" Coy
   of the 1/4th. Bn. East Lancs Regt. at the CLOTH HALL YPRES.

3. Dress for marching out:-
   Fighting dress, less greatcoats, flares, bombs, rifle grenades
   and entrenching tools (i.e. picks and shovels).
   The following will be carried in the packs:-
   Groundsheets, cardigan, one pair of socks, two days rations
   plus the emergency ration.
   170, Rounds of S.A.A. per man will be carried.
   6 Petrol Tins per Platoon and 2 Petrol Tins per Coy Hqrs, will
   be carried full for use in RAILWAY WOOD & LAKE FARM.

4. 4 Lewis Guns per Coy, and 24 magazines per gun will be taken
   forward on Limbers, one limber to each Coy, these will proceed
   at 4-0 p.m. this afternoon under an N.C.O. & one man from
   each Coy, they will then be dumped in daylight just off the
   Corduroy track, where mules were unloaded before, about
   I.17.a.85.90.
   They will then be got ready for immediate issue as the troops
   march past.
   Petrol Tins will be carried also on these limbers.

5. 1 Officer to be detailed by O.C. "C" Coy, with 1 Platoon of
   "C" Coy, & 5 N.C.O's "A" Coy. will proceed with the above
   limbers at 4-0 p.m. and will take over accomodation and duties
   in RAILWAY WOOD DUGOUT, he will report to the Adjutant 1/4th.
   Bn. East Lancs Regt. on arrival.
   The R.S.M. will accompany this party to detail the duties
   required and take over "Hqrs" accomodation.

6. Distance of 100 yards between half platoon will be maintained
   on leaving this camp for move forward, half platoons proceeding
   in file, special attention must be paid to keeping touch
   between half platoons.

7XXX All surplus kit to that being carried on the man will be packed
   in haversacks except greatcoats which will be rolled in bundles
   of 8 (eight). These with Officers surplus kit will be dumped
   on "Hdqrs" and Coy's dumps near Orderly Room by 6-0 p.m. and
   left in charge of Coy. Q.M.Sgts. The Transport Officer will
   arrange for their removal to Q.M. dump on empty ration limber

-2-

8. The Transport Officer will arange for one limber or maltese cart to report at Battalion Hdqrs at 7-0 p.m, for Battalion Hdqrs, and Medical stores for the line.
This is in addition to three limbers already mentioned in Para 4. required at 4-0 pm. for Lewis Guns.

9. Completion of relief to be reported to Battalion Hdqrs, RAILWAY WOOD DUGOUT.

10. All trench stores will be taken over and recipts obtained. These will be forwarded to Battn, Hqrs, as soon as possible after completion of relief, and before 4-0 am on the 14th, inst.

11. Acknowledge.

(signed)
Captain & Adjutant.
1/5th, Bn East Lancs Regt.

Issued by orderly at................

Copy No.1. "A" Coy.	Copy No. 7 Quartermaster
" " 2 "B" "	" " 8 Transport Officer
" " 3 "C" "	" " 9 War Diary.
" " 4 "D" "	" " 10 " "
" " 5 Commanding Officer.	" " 11 File.
" " 6 Signalling Officer.	" " 12. Spare.

- 2 -

8. The Transport Officer will arrange for one limber or maltese cart to report at Battalion Hdqrs, at 7-0 p.m. for Battalion Hdqrs, and Medical stores for the line.
This is in addition to three limbers already mentioned in Para 4. required at 4-0 p.m. for Lewis Guns.

9. Completion of relief to be reported to Battalion Hdqrs, RAILWAY WOOD DUGOUT.

10. All Trench stores will be taken over and recipts obtained. These will be forwarded to battn, Hdqrs, as soon as possible after completion of relief, and before 4-0 am, on the 14th, ins

11. Acknowledge.

Captain & Adjutant.
1/5th, Bn East Lancs Regt.

Issued by Orderly at ....

Copy No. 1. "A" Coy.	Copy. No 7. Quartermaster
" " 2 "B" "	" " 8. Transport Officer
" " 3 "C" "	" " 9 War Diary.
" " 4 "D" "	" " 10 "
" " 5 Commanding Officer.	" " 11 File.
" " 6 Signalling Officer.	" " 12. Spare.

Addendum No 1 to Appx. No 11

1/5th Bn East Lancs R. Order No 26

Sept 16/17.

1. Ref Para 4.
   Times for guides will be put back 2 hours.
2. Para 5.   For 9:30 pm read "7-30 p.m."
3. Para 6.   For 9:30 pm read 11·0 pm
4. Para 3.
   A Train will leave the YPRES ASYLUM SIDING at 3·30 am on the 17th inst. Accommodation allotted for 480 all ranks of this Unit.
   The allotment of carriages is 4 Officers or 8 ORks to a compartment.
   The Battalion will detrain at the second stopping place viz. level crossing G.11.a.9.9. at 3·30. Rear Hqrs will arrange guides to be at level crossing G.11.a.9.9. at 3·30 am, to meet coys on detraining.
   No Baggage of any kind is allowed on this train.
5. Hot Meals
   The Quartermaster will arrange for two cookers to be at suitable site within vicinity of siding at

YPRES ASYLUM by midnight. Mess orderlies will supply tea to the Coys on arrival at this point.

Care must be taken not to block the main road while issuing the tea.

6. Extra guides
O.C. "C" Coy will arrange for 1 platoon "C" Coy at I.6.d.9.9. to provide two guides to report to the Adjutant at RAILWAY WOOD DUGOUT at 10pm to guide two platoons of the 10th Bn Royal Scots to the embankment I.6.d.9.9.
The 1 platoon "C" Coy will however withdraw as per previous orders, only two hours later, that is 10 p.m.

ACKNOWLEDGE

[signature]
Capt & Adjt
1/5th Bn East Lancs Regt

Issued to all recipients of
1/5th Bn East Lancs Regt Order No 36
by orderly at 4-30 pm.

1/5th Batn East Lancs Regt   15.   1-9-17

UNIT	Total		Effective		Loc with Bde		Loc Detached		Sick		Arrivals		Departures		Remarks
	O	OR	O	OR	O	OR	O	OR	O	OR	O	OR	O	OR	
1/5.ELR	33	864	33	864	26	740	9	131	–	4	–	1	–	–	1.O.R. rejoined from Hospital
RAMC	1	4													4.O.R. Admitted Field Ambulance
ARM		1													9.O.R. To England on leave
A.S.H.		1													3.O.R. Rejoined from leave
R Rth Rgt	1111	1													1.O.R. To England on leave from L.T.M.B.
Chap.	1														
	35	871	33	864	26	740	9	131	–	4	–	1	–	–	

Locations of Detached
	O	OR
On leave	2	44
Attd B.H.Q.		12
Hospital	1	2
Attd R.E.s		26
M.G. Coy	2	8
Field Ambulance	1	15
L.T.M. Battery		2
III Army School	1	
G.H.Q Lewis Gun School		2
Brancardiers Camp Express		1
Sig. Coy		1
I Corps School		4
XIX Corps School		4
Depot Y Beata		3
Salvage Coy	1	2
Traffic Police		1
Town Major YPRES		1
Divnl Bomber Section		2
Attd R.F.C. course		
	9	131

(Sgd) G.G.H. Bolton Capt & adjt
for
Lieut-Col
Comdg 1/5th Bn East Lancs Regt

1/5th Batn East Lancs Regt.   30.9.17

Unit	Total		Effective		Nos with Bde		Nos Detached		Sick		Arrivals		Departures		Remarks
	O	R	O	R	O	R	O	R	O	R	O	R	O	R	
1/5 ELR	31	865	31	865	24	753	8	120	–	5	–	–	–	5	5.O.R. Evacuated Field Amb Struck off Strength
RA+1C	1	4													8.O.R. Joined from Depot Battn
ARM		1													1.O.R. Rejoined from Field Amb
1/1 S.H.		1													2.O.R. Rejoined from Leave
2nd Bdn Regt		1													3.O.R. Admitted Field Amb
WEST SURREYS		1													1 Off. to U.K. on leave from R.E.
CHAP															1 Off. Attchd R.E.S.
															Rev. Greaves admitted Hosp
															10.R Admitted Field Amb from Salvage Coy
															1.O.R. Admitted Field Amb from R.E.S
	32	873	31	865	24	753	8	120	–	5	–	–	–	5	

Location of Detachments:

	R	O	R							
On Leave	2	30								
Attchd B.H.Q.	1	15								
Hospital		2		7						
M.G. Coy		13								
Field Ambulance	3									
LTM Batty		14								
Training Camp Etaples	1									
XIII Corps School	2									
Sig Coy		2								
Depot Battn	1									
Salvage Coy	1									
Traffic Police		1								
Town Major YPRES	3									
Burial Section		3								
Sanitary Section YPRES		2	6							
5th Army Musketry School	1	25								
Divnl Sig School										
Cookery School										
Reinforcements										
Attchd R.E.s	1									
	8	120								

(Sd) Cecil Clare
Lieut-Col
Comdg 1/5 Bn East Lancs Regt

SECRET.

Copy No. 6

14.

1/5th. Bn East Lancs Regt ORDER NO. 42.

Ref Map   SHEET NO 4 Edition 1.
         Scale 1/10,000.   September 28th, 1917.

1. 'D' Coy will relieve 'C' Coy in the right Subsector of the OOST-DUNKERQUE-BAINS SECTOR of the Coast Defences to-night the 28th inst commencing at 7 - 0 pm. On relief 'C' Coy will withdraw to Battalion Reserve in Billets in OOST-DUNKERQUE-BAINS. (R27-C-85)

2. All details for relief will be arranged between O.C.Coys concerned.

3. 'C' Coy will leave 2 Lewis Guns and Teams to garrison M.G.Nos.1&2 Posts, who will come under the command of O.C.'D' Coy on completion of relief.

    The necessary interchange of Lewis Guns Teams for these posts will be carried out before 7 - 0 pm.

4. All Trench Stores (including Dixies) will be handed over on relief and Receipts obtained.
Original to be forwarded to the Orderly Room by noon on the 29th.

5. Completion of relief will be wired to Battn Headquarters.

6. ACKNOWLEDGE.

                                             Capt & Adjt
                                1/5th. Battn East Lancs Regt.

Issued by Orderly at 3 - 45pm.

Copy NO	1	'C' COY
"	2	'D' "
"	3	'A' "
"	4	126th Inf Bde.
"	5	Q.M.
"	6	War Diary
"	7	do
"	8	File.

SECRET   Copy No 2

1/5th Bn East Lancs Regt Order No 35

Ref Map Sheets 28 N.W. & N.E.

Sept 15th 17

1. On the night of the 15th/16th, the 1/4th Batt. East Lancs Regt, has been ordered to take over a portion of the front held by the 125th Inf Bde, from the YPRES-ROULERS RAILWAY exclusive to the ROAD which runs from D.26.a.3.0. to D.25.d.40.45. inclusive.
The inter Brigade Boundary will then run from D.25.d.40.45. to the Centre of WYLD WOOD at I.6.b.6.2. and thence to GULLY FARM.

2. Troops of the 1/4th Batt East Lancs Regt used to carry out this operation will be replaced by the Battalion as under
'C' Coy less one Platoon to I.6.b.8.9.
one platoon 'C' Coy to LAKE FARM.
'D' Coy replace 'C' Coy in RAILWAY WOOD DUGOUTS.

3. 'D' Coy will proceed by march route from YPRES at 6.30pm, via:- MENIN GATE, HELL FIRE CORNER, and thence by track to RAILWAY WOOD.
Four NCO's D Coy will proceed at once on receipt of these orders to RAILWAY WOOD

to take over accommodation in the DUGOUT from "C" Coy.

4. "C" Coy will clear RAILWAY WOOD DUGOUT by 8 pm and will proceed independantly to their new post. No guides will be provided for 5.6.6.8.9., but two Battalion Scouts will report to OC "C" Coy by 7.45 pm as guides for LAKE FARM.

5. OC "D" Coy will make necessary arrangements for Transport, direct with the Transport Officer.

6. Two days Rations & Water will be carried by all troops concerned in these moves.

7. "C" Coy on completion of their relief will come under the command of the OC 1/4th Batn. East Lancs Regt.

8. All Trench Stores, Ammunition etc, will be taken over and receipts given. Copies of these receipts to be sent to Batn Hdqrs by 9- am on the 16th.

9. Completion of reliefs will be wired to Batn Hdqrs which will remain in RAILWAY WOOD. "C" Coy to repeat their message to 1/4th Bn East Lancs Regt. (N.T.B. Station Call)

10. Acknowledge by wire

Capt & Adjt
1/5th Bn East Lancs Regt

SECRET   Copy No 11
1/5th East Lancs Regt Order No 36.

Ref Maps Sheets 28 NW & NE.   Sept 16/17

1. The Battalion will be relieved by
the 11th Bn (S) ROYAL SCOTS less one
company on the night 16th/17th inst, in
accordance with table under para 2.

2. Hdqrs, "A" Coy "D" & "B" Coys, less two
platoons will be relieved at RAILWAY
WOOD by Hdqrs, "A" & "D" Coys of
the Royal Scots.
"C" Coy less one platoon and 2 Platoons
"B" Coy at LAKE FARM will be relieved
by "B" Coy of the Royal Scots.
One Platoon "C" Coy at I.6.d.89 will
withdraw independantly at 8 pm.

3. On relief Companies will proceed
independantly to the ASYLUM, YPRES,
from which point they will train to
BRANDHOEK, Nos and be located at
RIDGE CAMP. G.11.a.4.5.
Train time table will be notified later.

4. Guides for the incoming unit will be
found as under:-
2 Guides (Bn Scouts) to report at
RED ROSE CAMP N.1.b.8.0. at 2.30 pm
for advance party to take over

duties and Dugout accommodation at RAILWAY WOOD.

4 Guides (Bn Scouts) to report at the ASYLUM SIDING, YPRES, at 6pm to guide HdQrs & 'A' 'B' & 'D' Coys of the relieving Unit to BIRR CROSS ROADS. These guides will ensure that the party proceed in the following order, HdQrs, "A", "D" & "B" Coys.

5 Guides each from 'A' & 'D' Coys will report at BIRR CROSS ROADS at 7-15pm to guide like Coys of the relieving Battalion to RAILWAY WOOD DUGOUT.

5 Guides from LAKE FARM will report at BIRR CROSS ROADS at 7-30pm to guide 'B' Coy of the relieving Battalion to LAKE FARM.

5. 'A' & 'D' Coys must clear RAILWAY DUGOUT by 7-30pm, but will not move back until relieving Coys actually arrive.

6 One Limber per Coy for Lewis Guns and magazines will be at the point where the light railway crosses the Causeway road about I.17.c.5.6 at 9.30pm.

Coys passing this point before the above hour will dump their L.Gs. and magazines and leave them in charge of a NCO & men.

who will load same immediately on arrival of the Transport.

All petrol tins brought into the line will be taken out and sent down in the limbers. The limbers will proceed direct to RIDGE CAMP.

7. All trench maps (paper) aeroplane photographs, sketches, trench and Lewis stores will be handed over to relieving unit and receipts obtained, to be forwarded to Bn Hdqrs immediately on arrival at new camp.

All trench stores must be collected into Coy dumps and every effort made to salvage as many of the stores scattered about the area as possible, even though they may not have been handed over to Coys.

8. Care must be taken that all vacated trenches, dugouts and camps, are left thoroughly clean.

Usual certificates of cleanliness will be obtained from the relieving Coys by Coy Commanders and from the Camp Commandant by the Quartermaster for the dump there. These will be forwarded to Bn Hdqrs at RIDGE CAMP by 9 am on the 17th inst.

9. Baggage wagons will be sent to the dump tomorrow at times to be arranged between Rear Hdqrs and O.C. Divisional Train ASC. No motor transport is available for the move

and if necessary first line transport and baggage wagons must do the journeys to the new area.

10. Bulk establishment of SAA, Grenades etc will be carried on wheels.

11. Special arrangements have already been made for the Camp allotted to be taken over by a party from the details under the orders of MAJOR KERR D.S.O, M.C. who is superintending camps and areas for the Brigade.

Rear HQrs will get into communication with the above Officer as soon as possible and ensure that all necessary arrangements are being made.

12. All Transport will move under the Brigade Transport Officer starting at 5.30 p.m.

The new Brigade Transport Lines are situated at YORK CAMP, C.5.d.0.4.

13. Guides for the Battalion on arrival at BRANDHOEK No 1 will be detailed by Rear HQrs whose time table of trains, when issued, hot meals also will be arranged accordingly.

14. 100 yds distances between half battalions will be maintained for march to YPRES, and in any marching WEST of YPRES, to BRANDHOEK there will be 200 yds

Issued by Orderly at 3 pm

Copy No 1   OC 'A' Coy
        2   'B'
        3   'C'
        4   'D'
        5   Rear Hdqrs
        6   Sig Off & MO
        7   War Diary
        8   do
        9   File.

maintained between platforms.
13. Completion of relief will be reported to Batt. Hd.qrs, RAILWAY WOOD. After all companies have completed, Batt. Hdqrs will move to RIDGE CAMP.
14. Acknowledge by wire.

(sgd)
Capt & Adjt
1/5th Bn East Lancs. Regt.

Issued. Sunday at 5 a.m.

Copy No 1   OC 'A' Coy
"   " 2   "   'B' "
"   " 3   "   'C' "
"   " 4   "   'D' "
"   " 5   BDE HDQRS
"   " 6   Major Kerr D.S.O., M.C.
"   " 7   Lt(?) Buxton & Scout
"   " 8   Sig Off & M.O.
"   " 9   War Diary
"   " 10   do
"   " 11   File

NOMINAL ROLL OF OFFICERS ON THE STRENGTH OF THE BATTALION. 30-9-17

LIEUT COLONEL O.C.CLARE. D.S.O.,M.C.	IN COMMAND	
MAJOR W.KERR. D.S.O.,M.C.	2nd " "	
CAPTAIN F.J.BUTTON	COY COMMANDER	D COY
" F.BRITCLIFFE	" "	C "
" R.P.HARGREAVES	" "	B "
" J.M.RAWCLIFFE	" "	A "
" G.G.H.BOLTON. M.C.	ADJUTANT	
" J.P.CARTER	COY DUTY	D "
LIEUTENANT W.H.BAXTER	TRANSPORT OFFICER	
" A.WADDINGTON	COMPANY DUTY	B "
" G.B.KAY	" "	B "
" W.R.MILLAR	COURSE	
" M.STEAD	HOSPITAL	
" J.FANSTONE	R.A.M.C.	M.O.
" A.H.FRANKLIN	QUARTERMASTER	
2/LIEUTENANT H.P.R.STANDEN	COMPANY DUTY	A COY
" W.H.HEWITT-DEAN	LEAVE	-A- "
" H.B.WORSWICK	COMPANY DUTY	A "
" R.A.COTTON	COURSE	
" P.G.LANCASTER	ASSIST ADJUTANT	
" C.CURL	SIG. OFFICER	
" D.WALTON	COMPANY DUTY	D "
" T.E.REED	LEAVE	
" J.HEWITT-DEAN	COMPANY DUTY	B "
" N.G.ORRELL	BRIGADE	
" A.F.PARKER	HOSPITAL	
" H.W.DICK	L.G.OFFICER	
" O.G.BARKER	INT.OFFICER	
" R.G.PARNELL	COMPANY DUTY	A "
" G.A.TURNER	COURSE	
" B.K.SLATER	COMPANY DUTY	C "
" W.PICKUP	COMPANY DUTY	C "

Confidential

WAR DIARY
1/5 LAN. FUS.

October 1st – 31st 1917.

Vol No 29.

Vol 9

28. G.
2 sheets

Army Form C. 2118.

WAR DIARY
or
INTELLIGENCE SUMMARY.
(Erase heading not required.)

Vol. 29. Page 1.

Hour, Date, Place	Summary of Events and Information	Remarks and references to Appendices
OCTOBER 1ST. ST. JOESBALDE.	TRAINING.	
2ND "	"	
3RD "	"	
MAP REFS. 4TH "	"	
BELGIUM SHEET 19. 5TH COXYDE.	Moved into CANADA CAMP for day and proceeded into front line W18.6.	H.P.
FURNES 1/60000 6TH NIEUPORT.	D Rgt-Sector of BDE front at NIEUPORT. relieved 16th H.L.I.	
COXYDE & 7TH "	8 FRONT LINE TRENCHES	
LOMBARTZYDE 8TH "	"	
1/20000 9TH "	" relieved by 1/7 LAN. FUS. and came back into support REDAN. nights of 9th and 10th.	H.P.
10TH "	"	
11TH "	"	
12TH "	"	
13TH "	FRONT LINE TRENCHES. night of 13th-14th relieved 1/7 LAN. FUS. in front line.	H.P.
14TH "	"	
15TH "	"	
16TH "	"	
17TH "	" night of 17th-18th relieved by 1/7 LAN. FUS. and came back to garrison the REDAN.	H.P.
18TH "	garrison the REDAN.	
19TH "	"	
20TH "	" night of 20th relieved by 70th MARINE REGT. and came back to CANADA CAMP W18.6. COXYDE	H.P.
21ST. LA PANNE	Billets in LA PANNE around FURNES X roads.	
22ND 25TH " 23RD 26TH " 24TH 27TH 28TH "	} TRAINING and Working parties.	H.P.
29TH 30TH 31ST COXYDE	CANADA CAMP Training and working parties.	

5 LF.

Please fill in map ref in Column I. thus :—
ref map sheet ____
scale ___.

and a cover should be provided stating

```
CONFIDENTIAL
WAR DIARY
OF
_____
NOV 1ST – 30TH
1917
VOL No ___
```

Please return Diary as soon as possible.

J. Clement

3.12.17

CONFIDENTIAL WAR DIARY OF 1/5TH LANCASHIRE FUSILIERS
NOV 1ST – 30TH 1917.
VOL No 30

1/5TH LANCS FUS.

WAR DIARY

INTELLIGENCE SUMMARY.

(Erase heading not required.)

Army Form C. 2118.

VOL 30. Page 1

Hour, Date, Place		Summary of Events and Information	Remarks and references to Appendices
November	1st Canada Camp COXYDE	Training & Working Parties 2ND LIEUT. C. CAULFIELD joined for duty	B.Y.S.
Wing Sheet DUNKEROVE (A) Scale 1/10000	2nd -	" 5 O.R. rejoined from hospital	B.Y.S.
	3rd -	"	B.Y.S.
	4th -	"	B.Y.S.
	5th -	" 2 O.R. rejoined from leave	B.Y.S.
Trench Sheet LOMBARTZYDE = 28TH Scale 1/10000	6th NIEUPORT	Front line trenches NIEUPORT SECTOR relieved 1/7th MANCHESTR REGT	B.Y.S.
	7th -	" LT. C. CLARKE + 4 O.R. wounded	
	8th -	" 2ND LT. SPERRY + 2 O.R. wounded 3. O.R. rejoined	B.Y.S.
	9th -	" 1 O.R. wounded, remained at duty 2 O.R. to Base 2 sick to H.P. 2 rejoined	
	10 -	In support in the REDAN NIEUPORT relieved by 1/7 LAN FUS.	
	11 -	" 3 O.R. wounded 13 sick to Hospital	
	12 -	" 6 O.R. sick to Hospital 3 O.R. rejoined 2ND LT F. CATTERALL posted to R.F.C.	
	13 -	" 1 O.R. sick to Hospital 3 O.R.	B.Y.S.
	14 -	Front line trenches NIEUPORT SECTOR relieved 1/7 LAN FUS.	
	15 -	" 1 O.R. wounded 8 sick to Hospital 4 O.R. rejoined	
	16 -	" 2 O.R. - 2 - 3 O.R. -	
	17 -	" Sug out at M 23 A 9015 blown in 2 O.R. killed Officers of 321st French Inf. Regt. came to look round sector	B.Y.S.

Army Form C. 2118.

WAR DIARY
INTELLIGENCE SUMMARY.
(Erase heading not required.)

VOL 30 Page 2.

Hour, Date, Place	Summary of Events and Information	Remarks and references to Appendices
LOMBARTZYDE Ed N 5 November 18th NEUPORT	Front line trenches NIEUPORT SECTOR relieved by 5th Bn 32/st French In. Regt. Battn went into BRISBANE CAMP	
DUNKERQUE	OOST DUNKERQUE, SGTS F. SHERRATT, R. HAWORTH & L/CPL SARHOADES proceeded to England to train for commission	F.Y.S.
19th TETEGHAM	2nd LIEUT H. WEBSTER 2 6R's wounded 12 6R's to Hospital Battn (less A Coy left behind to clear forward areas) embussed	F.Y.D.
20 - NORMHOUDT	to TETEGHAM, in billets Battn marched to NORMHOUDT, stayed in billets. 2 6R gained	
21st LE NOUVEAU MONDE	Battn marched to LE NOUVEAU MONDE stayed in billets & 6R's to hospital	F.Y.D.
22nd LONGUE CROIX	Battn marched to LONGUE CROIX stayed in billets	
23rd STEENBECQUE	Battn marched to STEENBECQUE, stayed in billets Lt P.H. McGRATH joined for duty 2.6R wk to Hospital	
24th "	TRAINING AFT Inter Coy Football matches 2.6R's wck to hospital 2.6R's to Base	
25. "	Church Services	
26. "	TRAINING A Coy rejoined Battn 4 6R's sick to hospital 2 6R's rejoined	B.Y.S.
27 - Mt BERNENCHON	Battn marched to Mt BERNENCHON stayed in billets	
28 - LE PREOL	Battn marched to LE PREOL relieved 8th S LANCS Battn in RESERVE in billets	
29. -	TRAINING draft of 12 6R's arrived 12 6R's rejoined	B.Y.S.
30. -	" L.G. firing on range at LE QUESNOY	

A. Holles ...
Capt 1/S
1.12.17

Confidential

1/5th Lancashire Fusiliers.

WAR DIARY — VOL. 31.

1st December 1917 — Pages 1 — 3.
31st   "   "

WAR DIARY
INTELLIGENCE SUMMARY

Army Form C. 2118.

1/5th LANCS FUS

VOL 31 Page 1

Hour, Date, Place	Summary of Events and Information	Remarks and references to Appendices
SHEET 36BNE 20000 December 1st LE PREOL	In Reserve in billets. TRAINING ie firing on range at LE QUESNOY	B.Y.S.
— 2nd —	Church Service. TRAINING. Ceremonial drill. Inter Coy Football Tournament. "B" v "A", "B" v "C". 1/6R HY. 1/6R Res. B.Y.S.	
— 3rd —	TRAINING ie firing on range at LE QUESNOY. Inter Coy Football Tournament final "B" Coy v "D" Coy. 1/6R to HQ. 1/6R attchd T.M.B. killed	B.Y.S.
SHEET LA BASSÉE 10000 36CNW1 4th CAMBRIN	Front line trenches from A27A 5745 to A27A 2085 relieved 1/7th Lan Fus. 1.O.R. rejoined.	
— 5 — , ,	2.O.R. rejoined. 2.O.R. on leave to England. 1.O.R. wounded.	
— 6 — , ,	4. O.R. rejoined	
— 7th — , ,	2.O.R. rejoined from leave. 1.O.R. proceeded on course. 1.O.R. wounded.	
— 8th — , ,	2nd LIEUT G. ASHWORTH & 15 O.R. proceeded on courses. 2.O.R. rejoined from Hospl. 1.O.R. accidentally wounded. 2nd LTS J.N. MITCHELL & N. MacARTHUR reported for duty. Enemy patrol seen outside own wire at A21d 7735 driven off by Lewis Gun fire.	
— 9th — , ,	2nd LT G.H. TONGUE & 4 O.R. proceeded on course. 5. O.R. rejoined. Enemy attempted raid on right front Coy of Battn on our right, but were driven off.	B.Y.S.

WAR DIARY or INTELLIGENCE SUMMARY

Army Form C. 2118.

VOL 31 Page 2.

Hour, Date, Place	Summary of Events and Information	Remarks and references to Appendices
SHEET LA BASSÉE 36cNW1 1/10000 CAMBRIN Dec 10th	Front line trenches from A.22.a.2085 to A.27.b.5747. Enemy patrol outside our wire at A.21.d.75.50 driven off by Lewis Gun fire. 2nd LT A. WALLACE reported for duty 16 C.R. rejoined relieved in front line by 1/9th Manchester Regt and	
SHEET 36BNE 1/20000 11th BEUVRY	In Billets. 6 Coy no reserve coy. Into billets at BEUVRY	
12 -	TRAINING in morning L.G firing on range at LEQUESNOY Aft Recreational training. 2ND LT A.R.G. BLAKE reported for duty	
13 -	Morning TRAINING Aft Recreational training. 2ND LT STIRRUP returned from course	
14 -	TRAINING. LT COL P.V HOLBERTON proceeded to England on 1 months leave.	
15 -	TRAINING + Recreational training in aft	CAPT N.HALL on leave to England
16 -	Church Services, after C.O.'s Service Major Gen A. Solly Flood presented Medal ribbons to Capt W.M. TICKLER. M.C. A/Capt A.B. SACKETT. M.C. 202152 Sjts. H. HALL. 202263. W. WALLISS. 200393 L/Cpl W SQUIRES 203402 A. DOLAN. 200393 L/Cpl W SQUIRES	A/Capt A.B. SACKETT. M.C. Capt W.M. TICKLER. M.C. 202387 J.E. HOLT B.J.R
17 -	TRAINING indoors (SNOWING)	
18 -	TRAINING	
19 -	TRAINING LTS A.C. HOLLICK & W.H RANGE returned from leave	
20 -	XMAS DAY Celebration MORNING Tabloid Assn. football Completion Tank Inf RE Engineers in final. 1 C.R. enjoyed at football 2 PM Coy dinners 5-30 PM Cinema. 16 C.R. on leave to England LT C.R. returned from leave	L.J.R

Army Form C. 2118.

WAR DIARY
INTELLIGENCE SUMMARY.
(Erase heading not required.)

VOL 31 Page 3

Place	Date	Hour	Summary of Events and Information	Remarks and references to Appendices
SHEET 36 NE 2/0000 BIEUVRY	21st		In billets. Coys Reserve TRAINING	
SHEET 36 NW1 LA BASSEE	22nd	Midday	In support. A,B Coys HQrs WINDY CORNER A8d 75+0 C Coy in KEERS Coy HQ HERTS REDOUBT A9d653S D Coy O.B.L A2b4q. relieved 1/8 Fife Regt	
"	23rd		A & B Coys. left/led working parties to 1/7 Lan Fus.	
"	24th		do do Gas projected from our front	
"	25th		Front at 7.30 PM bursts of artillery. M.G. T.M. & rifle fire at intervals during the night.	
"	26th		Working parties to 1/7 Lan Fus	
"	27th		do do Capt SACKETT. A.B. v. CAPT. HUNT. CHC in short leave to PARIS.	
"	28th	Pm Friday	Working parties to 1/7 Lan Fus. (Sorting front line trenches from A9d6715 to A3c8590. B Coy right front. A Coy Centre front D Coy Left front C Coy in support, relieved 1/7 Lanc Fus.	
"	29th		7. O.R. to 4.27 Field Coy R E attached.	
"	30th	"	Bottn H.Q. A9d8550 + vacinity of HERTS REDOUBT A9d6535	
"	31st	"	Shelled from 2-8.0. to 3.3.5 with 4.2"s & 5.9's Lieut J. WOOD. A Coy wounded, died of wounds at 33rd C.C.S. 2ND LT A WALLACE got to enemy line at A9b6354S Patrol from A Coy under 2ND LT A WALLACE got to enemy line of the Mahud Trench when B.Y.B. they saw a Bosch who fired a shot wounding 1 of the Mahud Bosch when B.Y.B. ran down dug out	

J.S. Wysark Major
Cmdr 1/5 Lancashire Fusiliers

Confidential

WAR DIARY.

of

1/5 BATT'N LANCASHIRE FUSILIERS

1st – 31st JANUARY 1918

VOL No. 32.

1/5TH LAN. FUS.

WAR DIARY or INTELLIGENCE SUMMARY.
(Erase heading not required.)

Army Form C. 2118.
VOL. 32. PAGE 1.

Hour, Date, Place	Summary of Events and Information	Remarks and references to Appendices
JAN 1ST GIVENCHY. Ref 36c N.W. LA BASSÉE SHEET.	Front line trenches. H.Q. A.8.d. 70.55. Battn. frontage A9d 65.35 to A3a 90.25. H.Q. heavily bombarded with Mustard Gas Shell.	A.Q.P.
Jan 2nd – "	Shaw caused gas to hang around – effects of it began to be felt by H.Q.	
Jan 3rd "	Offrs. (4 American atts.) & Men evacuated as gas cases. Battn. relieved by 1/7 Lan Fus. Came into Reserve at GORRE CHATEAU. F.3.b.50.60. Major J.S. Knycett-Rison R. atts 1/7 Lan Fus took over command of Battn. vice Major Es Gelle M.C. (wounded Gas) Capt. N. Hall took over duties as Adjt. vice Captain S.S. Jenkins (wounded Gas). Lt B.J. Brewer (M.O.R.C. U.S.A) was attached as Med. Off. vice Capt. Johnson.	
Jan 4th to 8th	RAME (wounded Gas) Training	
Jan 9th	GORRE CHATEAU. Working parties R.E. and to Support Battn – also training	
Jan 9th to 15th	Proceeded to front line – relieved 1/7 Lan Fus in same sector as above. Work done improving trenches, revetting, duck boarding. Protective patrolling, wiring in front. Sap & active sniping against enemy movement. Several O.R's met and Oth's claimed.	
Jan 15th to 17th	Jan. 15th Lt.Col. P.V. Holberton returned from leave and resumed Command. Re-organization of dispositions into deferred localities. Thaw after heavy snow made trenches very bad. Trenches crumbled in and deep in mud.	
Jan. 17th SHEET 36a S.E. HINGETTE	Battn relieved by 1/9th Man. Regt. marched in Bde. reserve into HINGETTE area. W.(II) Hol Berton to command 125 Bde. Bn. HQ. W.17c 90.50. Men APELETTE BRIDGE C Coy. in farms W.10 6nd. A. & D Coys in farms at LES CAUCHONS. W.6.	A.Q.P.

Army Form C. 2118.

WAR DIARY
or
INTELLIGENCE SUMMARY.

1/5TH LAN. FUS. Vol. 32. Page. 2.

(Erase heading not required.)

Instructions regarding War Diaries and Intelligence Summaries are contained in F. S. Regs., Part II. and the Staff Manual respectively. Title pages will be prepared in manuscript.

Place	Date	Hour	Summary of Events and Information	Remarks and references to Appendices
HINGETTE	Jan 18th to 25th		Training in HINGETTE area. Working parties to R.E. Stores to CORRE - 2 crops on even dates. Working party Tuesdays and Fridays. Loading coal RUAGE MINES de BRUAY.	A.P.
Sheet 36a. S.E.	22nd		Att. C. Corps Gas Demonstration with Div. Gas Officer.	A.P.
	27th		Church parade & inspection by 14th Br HOUGERTON Comdg. 125 Bde.	A.P.
	19th		Capt. E. A. ASH, Middlesex Regt. assumed duties as 2nd in Command. Capt. C.S. BARTON, M.C. R.W.F. attached for duty.	
CUINCHY Sq 36c. N.W. LA BRETE	29th		Marches from HINGETTE to CUINCHY sector in support. relieves 1/6th Manr. Regt. Bn. HQ. A. 20.c. Co. 40. 8 Coys. manning Keeps in Support to line battns. 1/4th Lan Fus Right Bn. 1/8 Lan. Fus. Left Bn.	A.P.
	30th 31st		Still in Support. finding working parties for 427 Field Co. R.E. and forward Battns.	A.P.
	1/2/18			

J. Meyres Major
Cmdg. 1/5th Lan. Fus.

125/42

VM 13

32.G.
3 sheets

CONFIDENTIAL

WAR DIARY of
1/5 Battn LANCASHIRE FUSILIERS

1st Feb: 1918   28/2/18

Vol No 33

Army Form C. 2118.

Vol. 33. Page 1.

WAR DIARY
or
INTELLIGENCE SUMMARY.
(Erase heading not required.)

Place	Date	Hour	Summary of Events and Information	Remarks and references to Appendices
CUINCHY. Sqr. 36c N.W. LA BASSEÉ	Feb. 1st		In Support line CUINCHY. Bn. HQ. A2c.60.40. Coys manning Keeps in support to line Pros.1/7 Lan.Fus. Right Bn. 1/8 Lan.Fus. Left Bn. Finding working parties for 427 R6 Coy R.E. and forward Res.	H.P.
	2nd		ditto.	
	3rd		ditto.	
	4th		Relieves 1/7 Lan.Fus. in Right front sector. Bn. HQ. A2.c.05.85. BRADDELL Pt. line held in defensive localities - hunt out supports - from BURBURE RYLET A27.B.40.30 to A22.a.10.95. Work done on defensive localities - wiring round - duck-aprons. Completed during tour, fire steps put in for all round defence. Several good patrols carried out through crater lanes to enemy ports. No casualties during tour.	H.P.
	5th			
	6th			
	7th			
	8th		Afternoon & 8th relieved by 1/7th Lan.Fus. and marched back to Reserve position billets in LE PREOL. HQ. F15c. 80.90.	
LE PREOL. 36 B N.E.	9th		LE PREOL. Finding working parties 1 by day and 3 by night for work up the line under R.E's.	
	10th			
	11th			
	12th			
	13th			
	14th		Relieved about mid-day by 1/10th Kings Liverpool Regt. (Liverpool Scottish), marched into "Rest area" at HOUCHIN. Bn. HQ. in camp. K10.C. 40.20.	H.P.
HOUCHIN. 36 B N.E.	15th		Training	
	16th		Training	
	17th		Training. Major G.S. Castle M.C. 2nd in command Capt E.E. Jenkins. M.C. Adjt. Capt. A.M. Johnson. R.A.M.C. and Lt. H.R. WAUGH. 46. D. returned from sick leave after wounds. Capt. A.M. Johnson (Gas),	
	18th			
	19th		Lt.Col. P.V. HOLBERTON assumes command of Battn. after temporary absence commanding 125 Bde.	H.P.

P.V. Holbert Lt Col
comg 1/5 Lanc Fus

33 K

Army Form C. 2118.

WAR DIARY
or
INTELLIGENCE SUMMARY.
(Erase heading not required.)

VOL. 53. PAGE. 2

Place	Date	Hour	Summary of Events and Information	Remarks and references to Appendices
HOUCHIN.	Feb. 20th		Training - firing 30 yds to Open ranges	
36B N.E.	21st		Training " " "	
	22nd		Training "	
	23rd		Training Baths - interior organisation. Cleaning of Blankets by Foden lorry.	
	24th		Large Wiring party of 400 O.R. wiring Defensive locality - Verquin K 6a.60.50. Church parade cancelled in consequence.	
	25th		Training - firing 30 yds to open ranges.	
	26th		Training	
	27th		Training	
	28th		Training	

N. Holtete Lt(x) X.
Comg 11/S -

B.
3.75

42nd Division.
125th Infantry Brigade.

1/5th BATTALION

THE LANCASHIRE FUSILIERS

MARCH 1 9 1 8

CONFIDENTIAL

WAR DIARY

Vol. 34

of

1/5 Batt. Lancs. Fusiliers.

1st – 31st March. 1918.

WAR DIARY or INTELLIGENCE SUMMARY

Army Form C. 2118

Place	Date	Hour	Summary of Events and Information	Remarks and references to Appendices
HOUCHIN Camp. Sq. 56B. N.E. K10 c.4.3.	MARCH 1st		Training. Musketry in Range. Assault course. Recruit Training etc.	
	2nd		Church parade.	
	3rd		Training. Platoon Competitions in Musketry, Assault Training, Drill etc.	
	4th		ditto.	
	5th		Cross-country running, boxing, wrestling etc.	
	6th			
	7th			
	8th		Church parade. Football in afternoon.	
	9th			
	10th			
	11th			
	12th		Training Competitions.	
	13th			
	14th			
	15th		The C.O. 42nd Div. Maj. Gen. Solly Flood presented medal Ribbons to Capt. Adjt. E.S. Jenkins M.C. N.C.Os and men of the Battn.	
	16th		Training etc.	
	17th		Battn. Field day. A Coy No.1 Platoon won the 15th Recreational Training Test	
	18th		Training etc. No.1 Platoon won the Brigade Efficiency Test	
	19th		Sig. Coy. musketry. Platoon mounted, Platoon dismounted at VAUDRICOURT.	
	20th			
	21st			
	22nd			
	23rd	11am	Battn. marched from HOUCHIN to LABUSSIÈRE on BETHUNE road and entrained. start 1pm, journeyed to ADINFER WOOD N.W. of AYETTE and bivouacked for the night.	
	24th	7am.	Lt. Col. P.W. Littleton and Lieut. H.R. Waugh reconnoitred the COURCELLES - LOGEAST RIDGE. 12.30 p.m. orders came to move at immediate notice. 3 p.m. Battn. left ADINFER WOOD for LOGEAST WOOD, bivouacked while 8 p.m. at Brickworks Cross roads. G.2.d.25.95. the Battn. 1500 by an the situation to front was not clear, finally orders came and Intelligence officer of 25th Div. left Battn. journeyed as far as light railway crossing 6.5.b. at this point the C.O. sent Nos. 11 & 12 Platoons of C. Coy under command J. Lieut. J.K.S. Page to BÉHAGNIES and SAPIGNIES to see if enemy were in possession. 127 Bde dis ensuite on the right. Report came back that allow was clear. The Brigade Commander (Brig. Gen. H. Jargues) ordered Lt. Col. HOUBERTON to take up a line in front of SAPIGNIES and BÉHAGNIES from H.3 Central where the 25th Div. were supposed to be still holding. The Battn. took up a line from the 75th Brigade 25th Div.	

WAR DIARY / INTELLIGENCE SUMMARY

Place	Date	Hour	Summary of Events and Information	Remarks and references to Appendices
SAPIGNIES RIDGE. 57° N.W. H.3 central.	25th		Attack and went in progress by 4 a.m. 25th inst. Attack on the left were attacked and the Battn. assisted in driving off the attack. About 8 a.m. all Coys reported that the enemy were massing in front of M.O.R.Y. Lewis & Vickers gun & Rifle & Lewis gun fire were brought up in front of the Battn. to screen his advance. An aerial machine gun fire. The attack came round the right flank of the Battn. About 11 a.m. Lt. Col. HOLBERTON himself went round the three adjoining units, Bing. Regiment with us in danger. A subaltern of the 1/5th Lan. Fus. was killed up and shown the direction of proposed counter attack. Meanwhile a message was sent to O.R. B. Coy., that the enemy was driving our third line Regiments. Capt-Adjt. F.E. Jenkins M.C. gallantly brought all available men of Headquarters and stragglers from other Regiments and led two to were taken post on the right of the SAPIGNIE road running through H.3.c. Capt. Jenkins was killed and his party broken up. Head. H.R. Waugh who was hit got back bag, an how late. After a counter attack by 1/5 Lan. Fus. After this about 1 p.m. news came that BIHUCOURT to the right were born in the hands of the enemy. Lt. Col. HOLBERTON then decided after getting into communication with Bde. to withdraw to the GOMIECOURT RIDGE G.6.b.5.5. to G.12.b.5.5. This was dug. C Coy. which did not get the message to withdraw owing to all means of being failing, till in right 3 p.m. when both flanks were found to have been near, than succeeded in withdrawing with fire on from the village of BEHAGNIES in the immediate rear, thereby successes in withdrawing with only slight casualties and rejoined the rest of the Battn. taking up a position on the left of the Battn. with the remainder of other Division again on the left, and about a Company of MIDDLESEX REST	Petty losses, casualties and men, about Remainder in getting back.
GOMIECOURT RIDGE E.	26th		about 100 yds to the left front, after this everything was quiet until midnight when was found that the troops of other Division on the left had withdrawn without warning the Battn. leaving a gap of about 800 yds. A strong patrol was formed of was left flank. W.C.d. HOLBERTON asked a Commanding Officer of MIDDLESEX Battn. to fill the gap. This was refused. At 7.30 a.m. the Co. Lt.Col. HOLBERTON received a message has been to Bde. to withdraw at 2 a.m. to a new position in support to 126th & 127th Bdes. who were taking up position near LOEAST WOOD. Lt. HOLBERTON has only had the message a two minutes when the enemy attacked the MIDDLESEX Coy. in front and apparently wiped them out, continuing their advance on our line. Heavy fire was opened in return, the brundt of the attack being borne	

1875. Wt. W.593/S26 1,000,000 4/15 J.B.C. & A. A.D.S.S./Forms/C.2118.

WAR DIARY or INTELLIGENCE SUMMARY

Place	Date	Hour	Summary of Events and Information	Remarks and references to Appendices
	27/5		by C Coy. The attack was held up but at this point the Battn became very short of ammunition. Lt Col. NELBERTON behaved in a very gallant and courageous manner going to and fro amongst the men in the open and encouraging them to spare their amm. and not to fire when they had a certain target. He was killed whilst doing this about 1.50 a.m. by a stray machine gun bullet. Capt Wm. TICKLER M.C. who has throughout commanded C Coy, now assumed command of the Battn, and immediately sent for Lt Col. Brewer D.S.O. Comdg ½ Lan. Regt who desired to withdraw at once to orders to Bde. to take new position. The 5th Lan. Regt to give covering fire to the rest of the Bde. About 2.10 a.m. the whole of the Bde. withdrew the Coys of the 5/5 Lan. Fus. The enemy charged this company about 2.15 a.m. only a few getting near our position and these were immediately killed. Someone seen to get round the left flank and LIEUT PAGE with one platoon rushed over to this flank and held them up. Under this covering fire the platoons commenced to withdraw from the right by sections and succeeded in doing this about 2.30 a.m. With only about 6 casualties after three days fighting. LIEUT PAGE with his platoon was the last to withdraw. The Battn then withdrew and joined the Bde. at 10 EAST CAMP on a west string. The wood, where stan of a few hours was made after which orders from the Brigadier the 5th and 7th Battns Lan. Fus. dug in on a line Ref. 57a N.E. Feb.6 is F27a - 21 c r.d. about 1 p.m. in support of 126 and 127 Bdes. All was quiet for the rest of the day and night. the 28th. On the 27/5 again all were quiet. At 4.30 pm. the T.O.S. Castle M.C. assumed and took over command of the Battn.	
	29/5		On the morning of the 29th the 126 and 127 Bdes were attacked twice and in both occasions beat off the enemy. Our Battn. was heavily shelled in the Support position and sustained about 70 casualties. On the night of the 29th the Battn relieved the 7/5th Yorks in the front line at L.3d. 9.1. to Bucquoy. ACHIET-LE-PETIT ROAD at L.4 a 4.0.	

PLACE	DATE	HOUR	
	28th		Battn. H.Q. L2b.10.80. C.Coy. in front line. B+A in support and D in Reserve.
	29th		In same position all day, in evening relieved by 2/5th East Surrey and came back to a support position in the Old German Trenches in GOMMECOURT WOOD advance along the east fringe of the WOOD in E.28.d.
	30th		In trenches GOMMECOURT WOOD. 7ts r8ts Coy Fus. in trenches in front.
	31st		Lt.Col. A.P.CLIVE. ♔ M.P. Grenadier Guards, took over Command of the Battn. from Major C.S. Castle, M.C.

A.S. Castle Major
Comdg 1/5 Lond Fus

10/4/18.

VOL 15

125th Inf.Bde.
42nd Div.

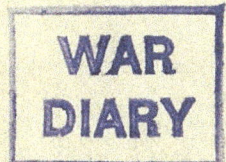

1/5th BATTN. THE LANCASHIRE FUSILIERS.

A P R I L

1 9 1 8

VOL 35

Attached:
   Appendices.

125/4 Vol 16

Huxcell 3H.G.
11 sheets

CONFIDENTIAL

WAR DIARY
of the
1/6 Bn Lanc. Fus.
Vol. 55
1-30 Apl '18

WAR DIARY or INTELLIGENCE SUMMARY.

Army Form C. 2118.
Vol 35. Page 1

Place	Date	Hour	Summary of Events and Information	Remarks and references to Appendices
BUCQUOY	1.4.18		The Battalion was in Brigade Reserve with 1/7th & 1/8th LANCASHIRE FUSILIERS in the line. Nothing of importance occurred during the day or night.	
	2.4.18		Digging YELLOW LINE mornings, carrying parties to the line.	
	3.4.18		Working on YELLOW LINE. Carrying parties.	
	5.4.18	10.0 am	According to message from 1/7th LANCASHIRE FUSILIERS, chasing enemy patrol "B" Coy. 1/6th LANCASHIRE FUSILIERS moved.	
		10.15 am	1/5th LANCASHIRE FUSILIERS moved into Brigade position in YELLOW LINE. "C" Coy 1/5th LANCASHIRE FUSILIERS ordered by LIEUT COL P.A.GLIVE to be prepared to counter attack if necessary.	
		10.25 am	Enemy reported to have broken through right flank of 1/8th LANCASHIRE FUSILIERS.	
		10.30 am	"C" Coy. 7th NORTHUMBERLAND FUSILIERS attached 125th BRIGADE so however were ordered to take up position 200 yards behind the light railway at F.27 CENTRAL.	
		10.35 am	All troops (MACHINE GUN Coy. LIGHT MORTAR Coy etc) ordered to stand to.	
		10.50 am	Message sent to 125th BRIGADE giving exact positions of 1/5th LANCASHIRE FUSILIERS in YELLOW LINE.	
		11.5 am	Message received from 1/8th LANCASHIRE FUSILIERS reporting situation obscure. Enemy known to occupy portion of their "B" Coy. 1/8th LANCASHIRE FUSILIERS are reinforcing their left flank through village of BUCQUOY.	
		12.0 noon	1/8th LANCASHIRE FUSILIERS report their reinforcing party to have reached MAIN ROAD through BUCQUOY and in touch with 13th ROYAL FUSILIERS on right.	
		12.15 pm	1/8th LANCASHIRE FUSILIERS asked for two platoons to reinforce their right. Nos. 10 and 12 PLATOONS, "C" Coy. 1/5th LANCASHIRE FUSILIERS under the command of 2nd LIEUT. W. STRINGER moved off to reinforce the right flank of 1/8th LANCASHIRE FUSILIERS. 2nd LIEUT. W. STRINGER.	

WAR DIARY or INTELLIGENCE SUMMARY

Army Form C. 2118.

Vol 35 Page 2.

Place	Date	Hour	Summary of Events and Information	Remarks and references to Appendices
BUCQUOY	5.4.18	12.15pm	Reported to Lieut. Col. O. St. Leger Davies Commanding 1/8th Lancashire Fusiliers who ordered him to place his platoons along a trench in the village. An officer of the 1/5th Lancashire Fusiliers name unknown reports 2/Lieut. So Ken 2nd Lieut. W. Stringer for a sergeant sent him to Rossex but a machine gun which was holding them up. This officer was wounded shortly afterwards.	
		12.30pm	1/8th Lancashire Fusiliers report they are holding line from main crossroads in Bucquoy on left to 13th Royal Fusiliers on right, but not in touch with any body on their left.	
		12.05pm	Intelligence officer of 122 Brigade, 57th Division reports their Brigade holding on.	
		1.35pm	1/8th Lancashire Fusiliers report their line now runs west from our cross roads at L.3.B.3.3 — 150 yards north and 250 yards south. They are in touch on the right now for two Companies of 1/5th Lancashire Fusiliers to counter attack through village.	
		1.35pm	Message received from the right of the 1/17th Lancashire Fusiliers and re-occupy line of 1/8th Lancashire Fusiliers.	
		2.0pm	Major G.S. Castle. M.C. is ordered by Lieut. P.A. Clive to see Capt. Sutton. 1/8th Lancashire Fusiliers and arrange counter-attack. Major G.S. Castle M.C. goes over to 1/8th Lancashire Fusiliers' H.Q. where reports to Lieut. Col. P.A. Clive that the situation is very obscure. That there is great confusion in Bucquoy - has all the 1/8th Lancashire Fusiliers Officers and casualties except Capt. Sutton. Lieut. Col. P. Clive immediately goes over with Major G.S. Castle M.C. to 1/8th Lancashire Fusiliers' 13th Royal Fusiliers' H.Q. which now together to arrange details	

WAR DIARY or INTELLIGENCE SUMMARY

Army Form C. 2118.
Vol. 35 Page 3

Place	Date	Hour	Summary of Events and Information	Remarks and references to Appendices
BUCQUOY	5.4.18	2.0pm 7.30pm	"C" COY inter-alia & "D" COYS 1/6TH LANCASHIRE FUSILIERS under command of MAJOR G.S. CASTLE M.C. go forward to counter-attack on left. LIEUT COL. R. CLIVE taking the right.	Situation Report attached.
		5.0pm	LIEUT. COL. R. CLIVE reports to be in advancing with three Companies. His report was handed to BRO. [Brigade] Hqrs. Handed to BUCQUOY at L.3.B.3.3.	
		5.30pm	CAPT. SUTTON & Commanding 1/6TH LANCASHIRE FUSILIERS reported wounded. 2ND LIEUT. COL. P. CLIVE to give important message. LIEUT COL. R. CLIVE sees over to him making having the message to himself. He left MAJOR G.S. CASTLE M.C. going forward with two platoons of "C" Coy. & Reb. to finish with 2ND LIEUT. W. STRINGER who is 150 yards WEST OF BUCQUOY-ABLAINZEVELLE Road, where 2ND LIEUT. W. STRINGER is killed. MAJOR G.S. CASTLE M.C. then pushes forward the whole line. Bets into Messages BUCQUOY-ABLAINZEVELLE ROAD, He then goes over to the left having orders with LIEUT. J.K.S. PAGE to push on. MAJOR G.S. CASTLE M.C. gets into touch with 1/7TH LANCASHIRE FUSILIERS pushing on with LIEUT COL. G.S. BREWIS. D.S.O. commanding 1/7TH LANCASHIRE FUSILIERS. Meanwhile "C" Coy had been an eye on the right, sought the road, never held up by machine guns & snipers & D Coy had been forced to withdraw on account of our own artillery shelling the main crossroads. MAJOR G.S. CASTLE M.C. then ordered the 1/5TH LANCASHIRE FUSILIERS to take up position in the village forming a defensive flank, with three Companies on line L.3.B.3.6. on left, where remainder/assaulted with 1/7TH LANCASHIRE FUSILIERS. The line then runs due WEST N.E. ESSARTS - BUCQUOY ROAD. Hence to L.2.B.0.5 until touch was gained with 13TH ROYAL FUSILIERS on right.	
			2ND LIEUT H. JESSUP was wounded and LIEUT. H.R. WAUGH took over command of "D" Coy.	
	6.4.18	6.30am 5.0pm	BDE [struck through] Everything normal except occasional sniping machine gun fire. Six Germans coming into village opposite the left post of "C" Coy commanded by CORPORAL G. HOWARTH, who immediately went forward told them to put their hands up + surrender, they then did so. He brought them in - four wounded.	

Army Form C. 2118.
WAR DIARY or INTELLIGENCE SUMMARY.

Vol. 35. Page 4.

Place	Date	Hour	Summary of Events and Information	Remarks and references to Appendices
BUCQUOY	8.4.18	1.55 p.m	CORPORAL G. HOWARTH brought in the enemy in — the other managed to slip away. CORPORAL G. HOWARTH then went out, taking three men with him to search for the missing rifleman. It was he in the stomach. He also granted was made very difficult owing to the enemy snipers and machine gun fire and he was eventually located. No.11357 PTE G CLARK J No.25331 PTE WHITTLE. ?, No.200 PTE HAZLEHURST and No.350 PTE ROBINSON Brought in CORPORAL HOWARTH. & also wounded. ? the 13TH ROYAL FUSILIERS who had been lying out since the previous day ? PTES. HAZLEHURST and also PTE G CLARK J were unable to get J yesterday they also assisted LIEUT COP. P.A. CLIVE'S body but were unable to get to him owing to sniping. All were, however, brought in under cover of darkness, clearing throughout, during this in broad daylight and with great courage. The enemy. No.4035 PTE CLARK J. has already received the MILITARY MEDAL for gallantry on MARCH 28TH.	
	7.4.18	6.30 a.m	LIEUT H.R. NAUGH commanding 'D' COY 1/5-7TH LANCASHIRE FUSILIERS, reported enemy advancing in three waves over ridge through L.4.B. He asked for artillery to be put down on L.10.A. and L.4.B. Artillery shewed on what ? completely broke up the attack. Enemy seen to be in very large numbers on old 16TH LANCASHIRE FUSILIERS' line. LIEUT H.R. NAUGH noted for his coolness on this line. Our "HEAVIES" go on to this line flattened it out. There was still a good deal of movement in and around the old front line but no forward movement observed. Nothing of importance during the day. The BATTALION was relieved by 2/5 WEST YORKS at 11.0 p.m. and marched to SOUASTRE where tea was provided afterwards embussed & proceeded to VAUGHE LES	
	8.4.18			

Army Form C. 2118.

WAR DIARY
1/5TH LANC. FUS.
INTELLIGENCE SUMMARY
VOL. 35. Page 5.

(Erase heading not required.)

Instructions regarding War Diaries and Intelligence Summaries are contained in F. S. Regs., Part II. and the Staff Manual respectively. Title pages will be prepared in manuscript.

Place	Date	Hour	Summary of Events and Information	Remarks and references to Appendices
VAUCHELLES	9-4-18		Battalion in Jumna horse lines in VAUCHELLES village. Men in French troops huts.	to GHQ Res'n
	10-4-18		Cleaning up. Coys reorganising and refitting.	
	11-4-18		Officers & parties moved to V. Corps School camp. Draft of 141 O.R. An new ammunition. Reorganisation. Inspection & two coys — England.	(Major) Divisional Corps Sports athletics
	12-4-18		Inspection of Bn by G.O.C. who Dros who spoke to the men and extolled during the great battle. Congratulating them on their gallant service.	
	13-4-18		Moved at 4.15 a.m. to WARNIMONT WOOD. S. (MUTHIE, ST. LEGER, RD. AND - Battn in field near bivouac. Bathing, training, & etc. and kits and Lewis Gun firing.	
WARNIMONT WOOD.	14-4-18		Church parade. Holy Communion. Commenced pioneer work on S. C/S. Saumur	
	15-5-18		Training — musketry & anti gas drill.	
	16-5-18		Preparation for forward up the Line - 5 p.m. Battn. marches out of camp - taken over by 13th Royal Dublin. 39th Divn.	R. K. I.

A7092. Wt. W125.g/M.293. 750,000. 1/17. D. D & I. Ltd. Forms/C.2118/14.

Army Form C. 2118.

WAR DIARY
or
INTELLIGENCE SUMMARY.
(Erase heading not required.)

Vol. 35 Page 6.

Instructions regarding War Diaries and Intelligence Summaries are contained in F. S. Regs., Part II. and the Staff Manual respectively. Title pages will be prepared in manuscript.

Place	Date	Hour	Summary of Events and Information	Remarks and references to Appendices
COMMECOURT	1/4/16		[illegible handwritten entries]	
	2/4/16			
	3/4/16 to 19/4/16			
	20/4/16			
	23/4/16			
	24/4/16			
	25/4/16			

Army Form C. 2118.

WAR DIARY
or
INTELLIGENCE SUMMARY.
(Erase heading not required.)

Vol 35. Page 7.

Place	Date	Hour	Summary of Events and Information	Remarks and references to Appendices
CUIGNEUX	1/4/15		Billets in CUIGNEUX. HQr & Coms. 19 Officers 511 Horses & 330 O.R. Details reporting at	405
	2/4/15		Cleaning up equipment, Battery	

M/Coste h/cal
C9/15 have tea

A P P E N D I C E S.

War Diary

THE DIVISIONAL COMMANDER'S SPEECH
APRIL 12TH. 1918.

Officers, Non-commissioned Officers and men of the 125th Brigade, in the Brigade I include everybody, R.A.M.C., Signal Section & Trench Mortar Battery.

'I want to talk to you for a few minutes with regard to the great battle which has now been going on for some time.

You have been fighting continuously for 17 days and you may like to know what the effect of your efforts was.

You took up a line on the night of the 24th March from ERVILLERS to SAPAGNIES. Your entry into the battle was most hurried and most unfortunate, but you did your part well and you held the line practically intact from the night of the 24th to the night of the 25th, until you were ordered to withdraw. Owing to the events that happened on our right and on our left it was necessary to order you to withdraw on the night of the 25th. This you did in a most orderly manner, a manner which is beyond all praise from a soldierly point of view, at the same time inflicting enormous losses on the enemy.

You then took up a line from BUCQUOY to ABLAINZEVELLE from which during the first two days, although you were not at first in the front line, the Division repulsed several attacks of the enemy.

Again at a later date April 5th, by overwhelming numbers they succeeded in taking from you some small corner of BUCQUOY. This, however, did not help him much and here we could deal with him, and you did deal with him. Owing to our numbers being short I decided not to counter-attack again that night.

Never mind, as far as you are concerned, your part was done and you did it well.

When I tell you that I am proud of you, that I am proud of the 42nd Division, and of the 125th.Brigade it is a mild way of putting it.

My feeling of pride and affection at the thought of the fighting that you have been through and the glorious deeds you have done, is far greater than I can express.

I put it to you that the whole Division fought like a football team. There were the Gunners and Infantry who fought, the A.S.C. who dealt with supplies and the R.A.M.C. who did not allow hardly a single wounded man to fall into the hands of the enemy, although we were withdrawing.

(2).

We were fighting for what purpose, the only one purpose that counts, the only one thing that counts in this war, to kill the enemy.

We have lost many comrades and friends but we have killed 6 times that number of the enemy, and I put it to you, that if you had not held on to ERVILLERS and SAPAGNIES and ABLAINZEVELLE, if you had allowed the enemy to break through he would have got AMIENS. He has not got AMIENS and all evidence proves that his losses were enormous.

Now I would like to tell you of the Battle in the North, near LA BASSEE. The enemy attacked there in very large numbers.
You may have thought that you were rather hard worked there on the defences, but the only defences that held were GIVENCHY and FESTUBERT on which you had worked. 700 prisoners were taken at GIVENCHY.

Now on a parade like this I cannot deal with the many gallant deeds that have taken place. The gallantry of which I read I know has taken place and before going into the battle again I ask the whole Brigade to adopt the Divisional Motto as I gave it to you and which has been read throughout the Army and in England "Go One Better".

Officers, N.C.O's amd men I thank you for your gallant services to your King and your Country. Your services are for your King & your Country and I am proud that you have carried them put in inflicting enormous losses on the enemy.

Now I wish I could tell you the enemy is finished, but it is no use saying so when I know it is not the case, he will attack again and will attack as heavily as before. I know as well as I stand here that you will do as the Brigade did before in the last battle and prove to the British Armies in France and the enemy that we can and will "Go One Better".

※※※※※※※※※※※※※※※※※※※※※※※※※※

SITUATION REPORTS.

received from IV CORPS.

Period 6 a.m. 6th to 6 a.m. 7th.

April, 1918.

G.352. 6th.

Situation AAA Quiet on whole Corps front AAA Some gas shelling of ESSARTS during night AAA Counter preparation on left and centre Div. fronts carried out from 4.30 a.m. to 4.45 a.m.

                                              12.10 p.m.

G.360. 6th.

Situation AAA Unchanged AAA Following details of fighting round BUCQUOY yesterday AAA Enemy heavily bombarded front and back areas from 5.30 a.m. to 8.30 a.m. AAA Line in front of BUCQUOY bombarded with heavy T.M.s and all our forward M.Gs knocked out. AAA Enemy attacked at 10.a.m. strength about 2 Battalions on 42nd Divn. front from right to F.28.c. held by Right Bde.AAA Left Battalion completely repulsed attack with heavy losses to enemy. AAA On the Right enemy entered our lines after severe fighting. AAA Counter attack launched at 4.30 p.m. by portions of 2 Battns. Right Bde. 42nd Divn. and 1 Battn. of Left Bde. 37th Divn. succeeded in regaining main BUCQUOY - AYETTE Road where strong opposition was encountered from enemy M.Gs. AAA Heavy fighting continued until late at night in BUCQUOY. AAA 4th Aus. Bde. and N.Z. Divn. were also twice attacked yesterday AAA those attacks were completely repulsed AAA All Divns. report very heavy enemy casualties.

                                              5.45 p.m.

G.368. 7th.

Situation unchanged AAA N.Z. Divn. report intense bombardment lasting 30 minutes upon 5.30 p.m.on AILLY-MAILLETT-SERRE Road from K.33.c.95.80. to K.32.d.7.8., AAA Repeated same intensely 7.30 p.m. from K.32.a.7.5. to K.27.b.7.9. AAA Enemy then seen advancing on junction of centre and right Battns. Left Bde. AAA Attack completely smothered by our artillery fire and no further infantry action followed. AAAA Situation quiet on remainder of front.AAA Prisoner of 17th Divn. captured by 42nd Divn. in L.3.central state enemy hold line in BUCQUOY by a series of posts AAA. Main line of resistance in our old line E. of Village AAA Relief of 17th Divn. expected in 3 days time.

                                              12.10 .m.

G.370. 7th.

Situation quiet and unchanged.

                                              6.a.m.

125th Inf. Brigade. (Rear)   5 copies.
126th Inf. Brigade.   "   5 copies.
127th Inf. Brigade.   "   5 copies.

125/42 Vol 16 VOL. 36.

35.G.
7chut

WAR DIARY.

1/5TH BN. LANCASHIRE FUSILIERS.

for

May 1918.

1/5 LAN. FUS.

WAR DIARY or INTELLIGENCE SUMMARY.

Army Form C. 2118.
Vol. 36. Page 1.

(Erase heading not required.)

Place	Date	Hour	Summary of Events and Information	Remarks and references to Appendices
COIGNEUX. Ref. Sheet 57d. J9a.60.40.	1/5/18		In Billets in COIGNEUX. Store in Farm J9a. 60.40. Firing down on range by each Company.	A.A.F.
	2/5/18		Day spent in preparation for proceeding up the line. 10.30 p.m. relieved 1/10 Manchester Regt. in the left sector 1/6 Lan Fus being in support. Batt. H.Q. being E.29.a.3.7.	
	3/5/18		Enemy artillery more active all day & night, firing Bursts of considerable enemy heavy artillery were slightly active during the day. Batt. Scouts covering parties for Scout Lieuts of Brigade H.Q. stayed up night.	
	4/5/18		Day spent in working parties remainder of Battn. employed on their Alarm posts & collecting salvage at B. Scr... Enemy artillery put a "Barrage" on enemy front line & supports. Brigade on our right to endeavour to endeavour an advance on our...	
	5/5/18		Line Herder the "Barrage" which stopped at 9.28.p.m. resulted operation was known up to 12.M.N. Enemy defensive fire received to the East trench and our Brigade on our right was not quite successful lost 2 offrs captured & Prisoners. 9 Prisoners, 2 machine guns and what from stood to the Coys marched into night m. 5/5/18.	A/S
	6/5/18		Day was spent in preparation to meeting attacks on the line. 9th Batt were relieved by No. 18 Comp S. Guards Regt.[?] advanced into Billets at COUIN.	a/s
	7/5/18		7th Batt were relieved by No. 7th Comp S.B.G. Regt[?] advance and to return continue and a again. Camp situated in the Woods. J2.a.2.w. Lgt L.L.G. Spent wash in cleaning up kit, men and Rifles & equipment.	a/s
	8/5/18		8/8/18 Lan. Batt after standing on the lines and cleaning up, sent the men on sick Rifles & equipment.	

WAR DIARY or INTELLIGENCE SUMMARY

Army Form C. 2118.

1/5 for Kus. VOL 56 Page 6

Place	Date	Hour	Summary of Events and Information	Remarks and references to Appendices
J.20.c.2.4.	8/9/16		Bay was spent in training under section commanders.	
	9/9/16		Batt: left the above Battle Positions & moved to hus Pats in the S. & then turned S. front over from Sherwd av. Bois to D.20.b.9. Batt H.L. being at J.21.c.4.9. at 4 a.m. & on came in position by 9.15 a.m. slept the night 3 the orders to our camp but no letters at all we due to our camp.	
	10/9/16		Day was spent in training under Platoon commanders. Lept was sent to Hospital.	
	11/9/16		Batt again took the above Battle Position. We moved off & occupied the same positions as on the 9th but in much better time, communication being established by 9.13 a.m. Sec Lieut Stafford & Everitt were wounded by shell fire.	
	14/9/16		Being Sunday, Church Parade were held. D Coy found as the cover a H.Q. formed a working Party.	
	13/9/16		Training.	
	14/9/16		Training.	
	15/9/16		Training, Batt targeted for trenches at 5.30 P.M. to march to the trenches by 10th Reds Bright (Extract 38/15)	
	16/9/16		Training.	

WAR DIARY

INTELLIGENCE SUMMARY.   Vol. 36 Page 3

(Erase heading not required.)

Army Form C. 2118.

Place	Date	Hour	Summary of Events and Information	Remarks and references to Appendices
J.2.a.2.h.	17/5/18		Batt Training on this date 2 Offrs & the 30½ O.R. were attached for training	
	18/5/18		Training with one or two Coys on working Party all day	
	19/5/18		Training with two Coys on working parties all day	
	20/5/18		Training two Coys on working parties	
	21/5/18		Training all Officers attended lecture by D.S.O at 6.30 P.M Divis Training School Staff	
	22/5/18		Training 1 hours night operations until 9.30 PM	
	23/5/18		Training ¾ Coy on working Party 2 Coys rest. 1 hour night operations on D.D.F Sand Trench & Dummy Wood Fld. & F.S. end Dummy aerial	
	24/5/18		Moved leaving all any two Coys working parties. Lecture for all Officers at 6 P.M. by Scout Offr.	
	25/5/18		Training with two Coys on working parties all day	
	26/5/18, 27/5/18		Areas Service Whole Commune for all Services officers. Working parties Training. Working parties. Recreation.	
			(Capt) (T/Major) G.E. CASTLE M.C. of 4 Gloucester Regt to be acting Lieut Col whilst commanding the Battalion from 20.4.18	
	28/5/18, 29/5/18, 30/5/18, 31/5/18		Training with two Coys on working parties all day. Recreation.	

G.E. Castle
Lieut Col Commanding
1/5 LANCS FUS.

1/5 LAN. FUS.
Army Form C. 2118.

WAR DIARY
INTELLIGENCE SUMMARY
(Erase heading not required.)

Vol 37 Page 1

Instructions regarding War Diaries and Intelligence Summaries are contained in F.S. Regs., Part II. and the Staff Manual respectively. Title pages will be prepared in manuscript.

Place	Date	Hour	Summary of Events and Information	Remarks and references to Appendices
COUIN	1/6/18		Training, two days on working party	
Req Huts? D	2/6/18		Church parade. B.E.C. Coy on working parties	
T2a 8.2.	3/6/18		One company working parties. Two companies battining as R.S.	
	4/6/18		Increase working parties. Firing on 30 yds range	
	5/6/18		"	
	6/6/18		"	
Sheet 57DN²E K19.c.6.0.	7/6/18		Battalion relieved 2nd Otago Regiment N.Z. and took up positions at K.19.c.6.0. as battalion in Brigade Reserve. Battalion under tactical command of O.C. 126 Inf Bde.	
	8/6/18		Dispositions of Coys "A" Coy K31.c.6.7. "B" Coy K31.c.3.9. C Coy T2.a.d.7.3. "D" Coy T3.a.d.6.3.	
	9/6/18		Improving positions	
	10/6/18		"	
	11/6/18		"	
	12/6/18		"	
	13/6/18		"	

Army Form C. 2118.

WAR DIARY
or
INTELLIGENCE SUMMARY.
(Erase heading not required.)

VOL 37 Page 2

Place	Date	Hour	Summary of Events and Information	Remarks and references to Appendices
Ref Sheet 57DNE 1/20,000	14/6/18		Battalion relieved 1/5 Manchester Regt. right front line of Left Brigade	
	15/6/18		Batt HQ K15.a.0.3. Disposition of Coys:- A Coy K21.c.6.1., B Coy. J21.b.2.9.	
			C Coy. K15.c.3.6. D Coy. K20.b.2.8.	
	16/6/18		K21.b.2.9. & K21.b.5.9. Shelled with H.E. & 18 pdr Shrapnel.	
	17/6/18		Four patrols sent out during night. Sudden storm at K15.d. 1.3. heavily shelled	
		11.10 p.m.	By enemy 9.20 p.m. – 11.35 a.m. 17	
		11.30 a.m.	Enemy line shelled 4.25.	
		10.30 p.m.	Enemy T.M. and Minenwerfer fire on VENA AVENUE K 20.b & K 26.a.	
	18/6/18			
	19/6/18		Intermittent shelling. Patrols.	
	20/6/18			
	21/6/18			
	22/6/18		A & B Coys relieved by C & D Coys	
	23/6/18			
	24/6/18		Intermittent Shelling. Patrols	
	25/6/18			

Army Form C. 2118.

WAR DIARY
or
INTELLIGENCE SUMMARY.
(Erase heading not required.)

Vol 37 Page 3

Instructions regarding War Diaries and Intelligence Summaries are contained in F. S. Regs., Part II. and the Staff Manual respectively. Title pages will be prepared in manuscript.

Place	Date	Hour	Summary of Events and Information	Remarks and references to Appendices
Ref Sheet 57N.E	26/6/18			
21.D.D.O	27/6/18			
	28/6/18		Intermittent shelling. Patrols sent out day & night patrols	
	29/6/18			
	30/6/18			

A.G. Catterall
Capt
M.G.C.

Army Form C. 2118.

1/5 LANCS FUS

WAR DIARY
or
INTELLIGENCE SUMMARY. VOL 38 PAGE 1

(Erase heading not required.)

Place	Date	Hour	Summary of Events and Information	Remarks and references to Appendices
Shet 57D NE I.20.d.0 BnHQ K14.b.40	1 2/18		14th day in front line. Frontage from K16.c.2.2 to K24.B.10.85. Bn HQ at K14.b.40	
do	2 2/18		125th Inf Bde was relieved & went back into Div Res. 1/5 LF relieved by 1/8th Mddx & moved to camp N of BUS WOODS	
Bn HQ J.20.a	3 3/18		Day spent in cleaning equipment etc & improving accommodation in camp	
do	4 4/18		Battalion bathing, carrying on with training. B boy burying cable	
do	5 5/18		B & C boys on working parties remainder training	
do	6 6/18		D boy working party at FORT BERTHA Remainder of Batt training	
do	7 7/18		A boy working in vicinity of J.35.b.55 D boy as yesterday	
do	8 8/18		B & C boys on working parties remainder training	

WAR DIARY or INTELLIGENCE SUMMARY

Army Form C. 2118.

1/5 LANCS FUS

Place	Date	Hour	Summary of Events and Information	Remarks and references to Appendices
SHEET 57 D NE BUS-LES-ARTOIS Billets	9/7/18		Battⁿ in comfortable Bus Whd at J20a. Capt WHITE K.R.⁵¹ acting adjutant. Incoming CO ¼ Coy.	
In Support	10/7/18		Reconn⁴ party to take over ends ⅕ L.F. to support R³BdeRe⁵. 8ᵗʰ L.F. support 7ᵗʰ right front.	
Batt H.Q.			Batt HQ in support CORK TRENCH Q.16.c.5.30. Coys in trenches C&D HQ in CHINCOURT CAVE B Coy	
Q1 c.o.5.50			at FORT BERTHA in J.34. Battⁿ paraded at 1.15 p.m. moved into BERTRANCOURT 1/5ᵗʰ LF	
"	11/7/18		relieved 1/5 MANCHESTER REGT. Relief complete about 4-30 p.m. Battn ½ mile NW of Army Huts Camp NEANE RATIC took over duties of H.Q. from Capt B.11.ᵃ.SS.15 (prominent to hospital) Large number of working parties supplied by Battⁿ while in support.	
			Coys working the following localities FORT BERTHA, SHRINE 12 and SHRINE W	
			MUSTARD	
d⁰	12/7/18		Battⁿ in support - working parties as above. Only slight enemy shelling on our areas. Measured shelling round Batt⁴ HQ and 4.2ⁱⁿ and 77 m.m.	
d⁰	13/7/18		Batt⁴ in support - working parties as for 11ᵗʰ inst. Quiet day.	
			Capt. J. ROUSE returned from hospital - took over duties of Adjt from Capt. J. WHITE (5ᵗʰ L.F.) Mᵉᵈᵗ. SERGEANT 1/2 Fld Amb reported for duty as Medical Officer Capt	
			NEAME returned to Fld Amb. Capt WHITE returned to 1/8ᵗʰ L.F.	
d⁰	14/7/18		Battⁿ in support - working parties as for 11ᵗʰ inst. Enemy searched localities hold by C Coy K.31.6.2.5 with 4.2 shells.	

J.S. Coste Ma/d
1/5 Lancs Fus.

WAR DIARY

INTELLIGENCE SUMMARY

1/5 Lancs Fus.

Army Form C. 2118.

Place	Date	Hour	Summary of Events and Information	Remarks and references to Appendices
SHEET 57 D N E 1/20 000	15/7/18		Batt'n in support. Working parties as for 11th inst. Enemy Artillery active about two shells round Batt HQ 5.9in. 4.20 in Q1a. Enemy aeroplane dropped three bombs near D Coy HQ J 30 c.d. about 5.15 a.m. no damage.	
Support Colincamps				
Batt HQ Q1 b 05.50	16/7/18		Batt'n in support working parties as for 11th inst. Quiet Day.	
do	17/7/18		Batt'n in support. Working parties as for 11th inst. Quiet Day. N.O. moving Cliff/5th L.F. would relieve 1/5th L.F. in Left Front. RT Bde Sector. Battalion Recounted slights burst of shooting on K31b, Q1b. Q1a. Capt. Page Lieut Waugh returned from leave in Paris. Our Artillery bombarded enemy defences for 2 hrs.	
	18/7/18	10AM	1/5 L.F. relieved 1/8 L.F. in Left Front Line (RT Bde Sector). "C" Coy occupied RT front went 3 platoons and one in support. "A" Coy occupied Left Front Line with 3 platoons and one in support. B Coy were RT Support Coy. D Coy were Left Support Coy. Front note kept by Batt'n HQ at K 34.c 30.70 & K.27.c 90.90. Batt'n HQ in Pioneer Trench. K.25 a 90.50. Relief was complete by 6 pm. Patrols were taken out from "A" Coy by 2/Lt H.R. Ronnebeck and Sgt Robinson to reconnoitre La Signy Farm in K 27 c.d. 2/Lt 2/Lt J.N. Mitchell "C" Coy Lt/Cpl patrol out. These patrols were out night 18/19. Burst of shelling during night 17/18 on K 33. K 33 a.c.	2/Lt W.H. James A. 2/Lt [illegible] A

WAR DIARY or INTELLIGENCE SUMMARY

Army Form C. 2118.

1/5 LAN FUS

Place	Date	Hour	Summary of Events and Information	Remarks and references to Appendices
Stat 3 JUNE to JUNE Bn HQ K25a95	19/7/18		Two patrols sent out to reconnoitre trenches K34a1890 to K34a2065 & K29d8595 to K28c43 respectively.	
do	20/7/18		Heavy bursts of enemy shelling on Bn area during day. Three patrols were sent out during night in co-operation with 1/7 Man. Regt & established touch (with them) at K28c0585.	
do	21/7/18		2nd Lt RONNEBECK investigated trench at K28c01 during day. He found a block in the trench. He was fired on by Germans. At 6pm a forward post was established at K29d8565.	
do	22/7/18		At 11am an attempt was made to establish several forward posts in front of our line. A post was established at K28c0205 & at K28c3055. 2nd Lt RONNEBECK & 2nd Lt MITCHELL & 2 other parties were unable to reach objective K28c1525 owing to fire from enemy post K34a3030 & K34c2095.	
do	23/7/18		A further attempt was made at 5am to establish post at K28c1525 in co-operation with Art & TM barrage. Two parties under Lt WEBSTER & 2nd Lt SMITH went for objective. When within 150x of post they were killed up by enemy fire. Lt WEBSTER was wounded.	

WAR DIARY
or
INTELLIGENCE SUMMARY.

Army Form C. 2118.

1/5 LAN FUS.

Place	Date	Hour	Summary of Events and Information	Remarks and references to Appendices
Ret SHEET 57NE 1/20000 Bn HQ K25a95	23/7/18		At 5.30pm 2nd Lt SMITH established post at K28c 2324 with little enemy opposition	
do	25/7/18		Capt D.J. STAYNER 1st Dorset Regt joined the Battalion as 2nd in Command. A patrol reconnoitred hostile post at K24a 34 & bombed enemy (2nd Lt ASHWORTH i/c)	
do	24/7/18		One of our posts at K28c 2095 was blown in by enemy shell fire between NOON & 2pm. Four men being wounded.	
do	26/7/18		125th Bde moved into Div Reserve 1/5 LF relieved by 1/8 Manr Regt. Battn moved into bivouacs between BUS & COURCELLES	
Bn HQ J22c55	27/7/18		Coys and bivouacs A at J23b Bat J28a C at J33d D at J22a Three companies finding working parties at Bde HQ at K33a 33 & at K19c 24	
do	28/7/18		do	
do	29/7/18		do	
do	30/7/18		do	
do	31/7/18		do	

SECRET. ADDENDUM TO   Copy No 17
Scheme for advancing our line 24/7/18

① **Add to para 2 Infantry**
A. Coy will also establish post at K.28.C.10.75
to be known as "A" post.
Post at present at LA SIGNY will do this at
Zero minus 1 hour, their post being taken
over on vacation by party No 1
C. Coy will also establish post at K.34.C.20.45
to be known as "No 5" advancing under cover
of banks along SERRE ROAD.

② **Add to Para 6 Organization**
Two Stokes guns will be put into front line
at A Coy's present No 1 post in SOUTHERN
AVENUE to barrage BASIN WOOD if necessary.

③ **Cancel para 11** Portion relating to CODE messages.
Artillery arrangements and communications will
be detailed at conference at 6AM 22/7/18

④ ZERO will be 11 A.M. 22/7/18

J. Thomas
Capt and Adjt for
OC 1/5 Lancs Fus

Issued with OO
distribution same as
for OO

SECRET   Copy No. 1

15th Lancashire Fusiliers
Operation Order No. 15

Ref: Maps. 57D.N.E. & 57D.S.E.   25.7.18

1. The 125th Inf. Bde. will be relieved by the 126th Inf. Bde. on the 26th July and night 26/27th July 1918. On relief the 125th Inf. Bde. will be in Div. Reserve.

2. 1/5th Lan. Fus. will be relieved in the left sub-sector of the Bde. front on 26.7.18 by 18th Manchester Regt. in accordance with attached March Table "A".
   The 3 new posts around LA SIGNY FARM will not be relieved until dark. Personnel for relieving these posts however, will be accommodated in front line until such time as relief can take place.

3. Advance Parties of 1 Officer or C.S.M. per Coy. and 1 N.C.O. per Platoon will rendezvous at B.H.Q. at 9 a.m. 26.7.18 and proceed to new area.
   Advance Parties will, after making themselves acquainted with new area, take over stores.

4. Tools, proposed work, ammunition stocks, S.A.A., Bombs, V.L. Lime, Discard Boots etc., &c, will be handed over and taken over, receipts obtained or protermas issued today and sent to this office by 9 a.m. 27.7.18.

5. Work Programme and full details of work will be handed over. O.C. "A" and "C" Coys will pay particular attention to this.
   Party of 4 N.C.Os and 48 O.Rs. found by C. Coy. for tunnelling at K.53.a.95.30 will be relieved by party from 1/8th Man. Reg. so on from the 2 o.b.m. shift.
   Carrying Party of 1 N.C.O. and 30 O.Rs. found by A Coy for above tunnelling party will complete their day's task.
   On arrival in new area working parties as on attached Working Party Table "B" will be found by Coys.

6. Rations for consumption on 27th will be sent to new area.

7. Transport Arrangements. 6 ordnance Cart to move limbers will be detailed and sent out as follows:—

   1 Limber for B and D Coys.   to report to B Coy. H.Q. at 2 o.b.m. loading up and go on to D Coy.
   1 Limber for A and C   to report at their Coy. H.Q. at 2 o.b.m.
   2 Limbers for B.H.Q.   to report 3 o.b.m.

   All material for above limbers will be ready at hours stated and after limbers are loaded they will proceed direct to new area.
   6 G.S. Limbers will be sent to J.30.b.7.7. by 4 o.b.m. 26.7.18 and there will await arrival of Coys. A Transport N.C.O. will be detailed to accompany same and ensure that they keep proper distances.

8. Guides. 1 N.C.O. from advance Party will be detailed by Coys. to report to J.30.b.7.7. at 4 o.b.m. 26.7.18.
   These N.C.Os will act as guides to their Coys. for new areas.

9. Completion of relief will be reported to B.H.Q. by codeword:—
   both by wire and runner.   "THANKS"   In addition, the relief of D Coy less the 3 forward posts will be reported by wire, codeword:—
                                          "STRENTH"

10. Acknowledge.

                                          (Sgd.) J. Jones
                                          Capt. & Adjutant
                                          15th Lan. Fus.

Issued at B midnight through Sigs.

SECRET.   Copy No. 1

"RATE" Operation Order No. 14.

Ref: Sheets 57° N.E. & S.E. 1/20,000.

1. This Unit will relieve "RANT" in the Left Sub-Sector of the Ride Sector on 18/7/18.

2. Coys. will relieve as follows:-

   "C" Coy. "RATE" to relieve A. Coy. "RANT"   Right Front Line Coy.
   "A"   "   B. "   "   "
   "B"   "   D. "   "   Right Support Coy.
   "D"   "   C. "   "   Left   "   "

   Lewis Guns & Ammunition will be carried by Lewis Gunners.

3. **Guides:-** One per Platoon will meet Coys. as under:-
   A & D Coys at 2:0 p.m. 18/7/18 at their respective new Coy. H.Q.
   B & C   "   3:0 p.m.   "   "   "   "   "   "

   Relief will be carried out by Platoons at 10 min. intervals, and should Platoons be up, by half Platoons at at least 200 yards distance.

4. **Advance Parties.** 1 N.C.O. per Platoon from A & C Coys will proceed to the line tonight, reporting to the Coy. H.Q. of the Coy. they are relieving. 1 Officer or N.C.O. from B & D Coys will report to the Coy. H.Q. of the Coy. they are relieving at 10 a.m. 18/7/18. These N.C.Os. will, after making themselves acquainted with their respective Coy. areas, take over and sign for Trench Stores &c.

5. **Working Parties.** All Working Parties at present found by Coys. will be handed over to relieving Coys. of RANT on and from midnight 18-19/7/18.
   Working parties found by Coys of RANT will be taken over as and from midnight 18-19/7/18.
   "A" Coy. of RANT will take over the working party found by C. Coy. RATE on and from 1.0 p.m. 18.7.18.

6. All Trench Stores, Maps &c, will be handed over and taken over, receipts obtained in duplicate and sent in to this Office by 9 a.m. 19/7/18. Bicarbonate of Soda will not be handed over but will be taken to new area by Coys.
   Water bottles will be left as full as possible and will be taken over as full as possible from RANT.

7. T.O. will arrange to send limbers to Coys as under to reach them not later than 1.30 p.m. 18.7.18. Guides will be supplied by Coys. for these limbers which must not be kept longer than necessary. As soon as finished with they will be returned to Transport Lines.
   1 Limber for B and A Coys.
   1   "   D and C "
   1   "   H.Q.
   1 Maltese Cart for M.O. to report to Aid Post.

8. Rations will be sent up as usual. Distribution Limbers as under:-
   1 Limber H.Q. Coy.
   1   "   A and C Coys.
   1   "   B and D "

9. Completion of relief will be reported to this Office by codeword:- "PARIS"

10. Acknowledge.

                                                           (Sgd.) J. Cause.
                                                           Capt. & Adjutant.
                                                                "RATE"

17/7/18

Issued at 10.0 p.m. through Signals.

Scheme for advancing our line

21.7.10

Ref SY D NE 1/20000

1. **Object** to establish a line of posts in advance of our present front line to conform with line now held by Battalion on our left.

2. **Situation** Posts to be established at:-
   (1) K 28 c 26
   (2) K 28 c 12 (junction of SOUTHERN AVENUE and enemy line)
   (3) K 34 A 25 60 (junction of NEW GATE and enemy front line)
   (4) K 34 A 25 30 (junction of hedge and enemy front line)

3. **Plan.** A Coy will establish posts 1 and 2.
   C Coy will establish posts 3 and 4.
   All parties assaulting to be 1 NCO and 5 OR. Stong pts 2 and 3 parties to have an officer.
   All assaulting parties to man at ZERO.

   No 1 post at K 28 c 26 will be established by line of approach down old trench from LA SIGNY FARM at K 27 D 86.

   No 2 post at K 28 c 12 by line of approach down SOUTHERN AVENUE.

   No 3 post at K 34 A 25 60 by line of advance down NEWGATE ST.

   No 4 post K 34 A 25 30 by approach down hedge.

4. **Gear** Assaulting parties will wear drill order with entrenching tools each man to carry 120 rounds SAA and 2 bombs (one in each side pocket of jacket) S.B.R. at alert rifles loaded (5 rounds) bayonets fixed 1 pick and 2 others per party 4 sandbags per man.

5. **Consolidation**
   No 1 party on reaching objective will work down enemy trench as far as possible to its right and establish block.

   No 2 party will establish block in SOUTHERN AVENUE and will work down enemy trench to its right as far as possible and establish a second block.

   No 3 and No 4 parties will establish blocks on either flank & forward working down enemy trenches as far as possible.

(12) ACKNOWLEDGE.

fao. J5 [signature]
Capt Sleigh
1/5 Linc Fus

Issued through Sigs at 12 midnight 21/1/6
Distribution: -
Copy No. 1 GOC
         2 A Coy
         3 B Coy
         4 C
         5 D
         6 H.Q. and S.O. S.A.A.
         7 Inf Bde Bn
         8 1/4 Lanc Fus
         9 1/5 Man Regt
        10 Adjt File
        11 War Diary
        12

SECRET.

Copy No. 1
25-X-18

Honorable "A" Sector on conjunction with O.O. No. 18.

SERIAL NO.	UNIT	RELIEVED BY	TAKEN OVER ON RELIEF FROM	GUIDES	REMARKS
1	A Coy 8th Can. Inf.	B Coy 9th Man. Reg.	A Coy 8th Man. Bat.	1 O.R. Unknown	Advance party of Officers and N.C.O. Co Station of 8th Man. Bat. arriving 10 a.m. 25-X-18
2	B	D	B	1 O.R. 8th Man. B.Q. will accompany	Advance party of 1 Officer and 1 N.C.O. per Station 8th Man. Bat. reporting morning 25-X-18
3	C	A	C	1 N.C.O. and 2 O.R. from B Coy. 8th	Advance party of 1 Officer and 1 N.C.O. per Station 9th Man. Bat. reporting 9 a.m. 26-X-18
4	D	C	D		Advance party of 1 Officer and 1 N.C.O. per Station 9th Man. Bat. reporting morning 25-X-18
5	H.Q.	H.Q.	H.Q.	Guide & Guide COLLINGCAMPS CHURCH at 3.30 p.m.	

Except No. 2 all Companies Relieved will be relieved by CREEROY AV and AVENUE no. 1.38 a J. to 6 and S.Q. at......... Co. 2 thence by road to B.Q.
ROUNAY AV.

No. 143

Note: — Units on relieved by will then be related to red flags on barbed wire areas as made in Cambles no road will be used during relief.
No fires to be lit in mean time until otherwise stated.

Capt I. Stone
Ent. 4 Standard
10 Can. Inf.

SECRET

Copy No. 1
25.7.18.

Work on Carr-with-Bush in connection with
18th Bn 1st OO No. 15.

The following working parties will be taken over by this Bn'd at 2.30 pm. 26.7.18.

SERIAL NO.	STRENGTH.	REPORT TO.	TIME.	PLACE.	NATURE OF WORK.	WORK CEASES.	TO BE FOUND BY.
1.	3 Офс. у 60 О.R. (3 shifts of 1 Офс. and 20 ORs.)	179 Canad. Engrs. R.B.	7.30 a.m. 3.30 p.m. 11.30 p.m.	T.19.a.n.2.	Work on Pile E.O. Shift 5 to 6 at railway Commenced. No 3 taken shift 26.7.18.		C. Coy.
4.	3 Офс. у 60 О.R. (3 shifts of 1 Офс. and 20 ORs. each)	262 Canad. Engrs. P.B.	6.30 a.m. 2.30 p.m. 10.30 p.m.	T.22.a. 3.3.	Beyond HOOGE SWITCH.	3 Canad.	A. Coy.
5.	3 Офс. у 60 О.R. (3 shifts of 1 Офс. and 20 ORs. each)	E. Section 179 Canad. Engrs. R.B.	6.30 a.m. 2.30 p.m. 10.30 p.m.	Bttn. E.O. on road at T.24.n.6.9.	Both E.O. R.19.c.2.n.	3 Canad.	B. Coy.

TO BE RETAINED.

(Sgd) Johns
Col't. J. Astarland
18th Bn. Can. Inf.

Army Form C. 2118.

WAR DIARY
or
INTELLIGENCE SUMMARY.
(Erase heading not required.)

1/5 LANCASHIRE FUSILIERS

FROM:- 1st AUGUST 1918
TO :- 31st AUGUST 1918

VOLUME No. 39

CONFIDENTIAL

Page 1 Volume 39

1/5 LAN. FUS

WAR DIARY
or
INTELLIGENCE SUMMARY.

Army Form C. 2118.

Place	Date	Hour	Summary of Events and Information	Remarks and references to Appendices
Ref Sheet 57d NE				
Bn HQ at J22c55	1/8/18		Minden Day. Each man wore red rose. Brigade parade for presentation of awards by the Divisional Commander. Battalion Sports held in the afternoon	
do	2/8/18		Boys on working parties	
Bn HQ K20b15y53	3/8/18		1/5th L.F. relieved 1/6. Manr Regt on left batt, left Bde front. Relief was complete by 11pm	
do	4/8/18		C coy in front line on left occupying posts in K22 a & b. A boy on night in posts in K22 c & d. D in support. B in reserve	
do	5/8/18		2nd Lt Riley & 4 O.R. were sent out to reconnoitre RED COTTAGE K28a 36.25. They left post at K28 a & 8 at 5.35 pm & made their way to RED COTTAGE & found the greater part of the way to the enemy. They found objective unoccupied. Three patrols went out in daylight but did not get any important information	
do	6/8/18		B & D boys relieved C & A boys in the front line	
do	7/8/18			
do	8/8/18	3.0 pm	A patrol consisting of 2nd Lt STOTT & 3 O.R. went along NORTHERN AVENUE K28a to find if post at K28 b0b5 was held by the enemy. They got over a barricade & then saw a German sentry 15 yds away. 2nd Lt STOTT exposed himself & was shot through the head. Another member of the patrol in an endeavour to get 2nd Lt Stott away was shot at, a bullet passing through his sleeve	

WAR DIARY
INTELLIGENCE SUMMARY

Page 2 Volume 1/5 Lan Fus. Army Form C. 2118.

Place	Date	Hour	Summary of Events and Information	Remarks and references to Appendices
SHEET 57d NE				
B.HQ K20d 15.75	8/8/18	contd	The patrol then had to retire leaving the body when it lay	
do	9/8/18		Our patrols went out during daylight but did not get in touch with enemy	
do	10/18		Sgt Smith & 3 men went out on patrol in the afternoon. They examined TOUVENT FARM & then went on to STAFF COPSE without finding the enemy. They took up a position some distance S of STAFF COPSE & waited until dusk. At 9.15pm they saw between 30 & 40 Germans coming down MONK.TR. K.8.b. These Germans saw our patrol & made for them but Sgt SMITH & his patrol got back safely after inflicting several casualties on the enemy	
do	11/8/18		The 1/5 L.F. was relieved by 1/4th L.F. & moved back into Brigade Reserve	
B.HQ J14d.60.85	12/8/18		A coy at K20d. B at J30 b & 32d. C at K19 a & c. D at K13 d & K11 & c	
	13/8/18		do	
	14/8/18		Enemy withdrew in an easterly direction 1/4/18 Lan Fus pushed forward keeping them in touch. B coy 1/5 Lan Fus moved up to FORT HOD K21a 3.6	
B.HQ K25.b.00.75	15/8/18		Battn H.Q in PIONEER TR. A coy in FORT STEWART. B in FORT HOD C in K20 c D in PAPEN TR K21 b & c	

Page 3 Volume

1/5 LAN. FUS.

WAR DIARY or INTELLIGENCE SUMMARY
Army Form C. 2118.

Place	Date	Hour	Summary of Events and Information	Remarks and references to Appendices
Ref Sheet 57^DNE				
BHQ K25 b00 45	16/8/18		Companies in same localities as 15th inst. Company training etc	
do	17/8/18		ditto	
do	18/8/18		ditto	
do	19/8/18		Officers reconnoitred ground in front of SERRE. A conference held in the evening to discuss coming Operations	
do	20/8/18		BHQ moved to MUNICH TR K36a78. Coys moved to assembly positions W of BEAUCOURT PUISIEUX RD.	
BHQ K36a78	21/8/18	4.45am	D, A & C. Coys attacked enemy position on HILL 140 L26 & 32. They advanced through a thick mist with only slight casualties behind our creeping barrage. Objective was taken.	
		6.55 am	B Coy advanced through 1st Objective & took 2nd Objective along road L27 b 9 2. Touch was established with New Zealand Div on left & 127 Bde on right. Enemy sniping active	
do	22/8/18	5.0 am	Position was held during day. Enemy counterattacked behind a barrage. He was driven off & prisoners were taken	
		4.0 pm	Enemy again counterattacked but was caught in his own barrage as well as ours	

Page 4 Volume.

1/5 LAN. FUS.

WAR DIARY or INTELLIGENCE SUMMARY

Army Form C. 2118.

Place	Date	Hour	Summary of Events and Information	Remarks and references to Appendices
Ref Sheet 57 NE				
BHQ K36 a 48	23/8/18		Battalion in support on hill 140. Day passed fairly quietly	
BHQ K29 b 07	24/8/18		Battalion relieved by 1/8th Manchesters & coys marched back to squares K29 c & d K30 a & c W. of SERRE. Battalion rested during day. At 10 pm battalion moved E of SERRE to K25 a 83. Total prisoners taken 84. Casualties 20 killed 8 missing 66 wounded	10 off killed [crossed out] 1 off wounded 1 killed
BHQ K25 a 83	25/8/18		Day spent in re-organising etc. At 6 pm Battalion marched to MIRAUMONT & bivouced in field L34 b 51.	
BHQ L35 a 83	26/8/18		Battalion making living accommodation & cleaning up	
— do —	27/8/18		Coys inspected by CO. At 4.30 pm Batt marched to G33 d in Divisional Reserve	
Ref Sheet 57e NW & SW.			Battalion nearly all slept in the open in the rain.	
BHQ G33 c 23.	28/8/18		BCD coys moved into ravine G33 c 35. All ranks making accommodation	
do	29/8/18		Enemy reported withdrawing E of BAPAUME	
do	30/8/18		All companies training	
—	31/8/18		Batt relieved 1/8th Man Regt. 1/125th Bde in support behind 127th Bde. Bn HQ at M5 a 2065. A coy M4 b 66. B at M5 c 5.3. C at M4 d 88. D at M4 b 59	[signature] R.G. Castle Lt Col Comm 1/5 L.F.

WAR DIARY

1/5 LAN. FUS.

SEPTEMBER 1918

VOL. 40.

Army Form C. 2118.

PAGE 1

WAR DIARY
or
INTELLIGENCE SUMMARY.

VOL 40   1/5 LAN. FUS.

(Erase heading not required.)

Place	Date	Hour	Summary of Events and Information	Remarks and references to Appendices
REF 57c BHQ M5.d.20.65	1/9/18		125 Bde in support to 129 Bde. Battalion in trenches in M.4.b.6.d. & M.5.c.	
	2/9/18	10.30 am	Battalion was attached to 129 Bde & took over positions N of THILLOY from 1/8 Lan Fus. BHQ. N.1.a.55. boys billeted in N.2.b.	
N.1a.55.		8.30 pm	Battalion again moved forward taking over positions about REINCOURT from 1/8 Lan Fus who moved forward BHQ N.4.d.69 Two boys E of REINCOURT N6.c N.11.b. N.12.a. with support boys in N.5. Batt in support to 1/8 Lan Fus in front line	
N.4.d.69.	3/9/18		The enemy again retiring during the night the Battalion moved at 11am to take up positions on high ground E of VILLERS-AU-FLOS At 5pm moved again to positions on high ground W of BUS in support to 1/5 Lan Fus. Leaving 1/8 to follow BHQ O.23.d.6.4. At 10.30 pm orders came through for 1/5 Lan Fus to forward next morning at 7am & continue the advance	47
	4/9/18	12.1 am	boys moved to assembly positions W of railway in P.19.b & d & P.26 a & c BHQ remaining at O.23.d.64	
		4.0 am	C & B boys pushed forward to make good high ground on good line between P.21.27 & P.22.28. B boy was held up by MGs & barrage & lost all

PAGE 2　　　　　　WAR DIARY　　　　　　Army Form C. 2118.
VOL. 40　　　　　　　　or
　　　　INTELLIGENCE SUMMARY.　　　1/5 LAN FUS.

Place	Date	Hour	Summary of Events and Information	Remarks and references to Appendices
	4/9/18 cont'd		Officers but one (1 killed 2 wounded) A line was established by B Coy in trench P.27.d.d.4 on the left 300x E of CANAL DU NORD	
		11.0 am	BHQ moved up to railway embankment P.20.c.0.9	
		9.0 pm	C Coy on left. D Coy in night attacked behind barrage. D Coy were held up but C Coy reached NEUVILLE BOURJONVAL gaining touch with NZ Div on left. B Coy got into touch with 4th Lincolns 17th Div on right.	
	5/9/18		At dawn B Coy pushed forward posts to Lench Tramway P.22.c. A Coy establishing posts in village in front of C Coy. Our positions were heavily shelled during day & again between 9pm & midnight. Gas shells were used.	
	6/9/18	10am	N.Z. Div took over our positions	
		5pm	Coy received orders to march back. They marched to BARASTRE & were taken on lorries to PYS. Batt quartered in ravine G.33.c	
			Casualties during operations:	
			Killed — 1 off, 4 O.R.　Wounded — 4 off, 58 O.R.	

VOLUME 40

PAGE 3

1/5 LAN. FUS.

Army Form C. 2118.

WAR DIARY
or
INTELLIGENCE SUMMARY.
(Erase heading not required.)

Place	Date	Hour	Summary of Events and Information	Remarks and references to Appendices
Ref 57cNWI.20500				
BHQ G.33.c.14	7/9/18		Battalion in RAVINE G.33.c. Resting + re-organising 42nd Div in Corps Reserve	
"	8/9/18		2nd day of rest	
"	9/9/18		3rd day of rest. Lt Colonel CASTLE went on leave. Major STAYNER assumed command	
"	10/9/18		Battalion training	
"	11/9/18		Battalion training	
"	12/9/18		Battalion training	
	13/9/18		A & D Coys tactical exercises, remainder training, firing on range etc	
	14/9/18		B & C. route march + tactical scheme, remainder training	
	15/9/18		Church Parade	
	16/9/18		A Coy tactical exercise remainder training	
	17/9/18		Batt went to Tank Demonstration N of IRLES	
	18/9/18		B + C Coys route march to HILL 140 L.29. + tactical exercise	
	19/9/18		Training. Making new bivouacs	
	20/9/18		Training. Making new bivouacs	
	21/9/18		Inspections etc before moving into the line	
	22/9/18		42nd Div relieved 37th Div in line E of HAVRINCOURT + TRESCAULT. 1/5 Lan Fus.	

Page 4 VOLUME 40 WAR DIARY 1/5 LAN. FUS. Army Form C. 2118.

or

INTELLIGENCE SUMMARY.

Place	Date	Hour	Summary of Events and Information	Remarks and references to Appendices
REF 57c NW + SW	22/9/18	cont'd	marched to BEUGNY & relieved 8th Lines Regt. 125th Bde in Divisional Reserve.	
57c NE + SE			BHQ I 22 a 05. Coys billeted close by. Enemy shelled Batt area with long range gun during the night	
BHQ I22a05	23/9/18		Battalion improving billets & cleaning up area. Coy Cmdrs & C.O. reconnoitred forward areas.	
"	24/9/18		B & C Coys went to Baths at VELU	
ditto	25/9/18		C.O. & Coy Cmdrs reconnoitred forward area. Lt Col G.S. CASTLE returned from leave & took command of battalion	
	26/9/18		At 19.00 hrs Battalion marched from BEUGNY to LEBOUCQUIERE & at 20.30 hrs were taken to RUYAULCOURT in lorries. Battalion marched to TRESCAULT via METZ. The METZ – TRESCAULT road was heavily shelled & several men hit. The battalion took up positions in trenches about Q10 central. BHQ at Q10d05	
	27/9/18	08.34	1/4 1/8 Lan Fus attacked in order to take BEAUCAMP RIDGE	
		09.20	1/5 Lan Fus moved up. D & C Coys went into SHERWOOD AVENUE & SNAP TRENCH B Coy remained by BHQ. A Coy moved close to BILHEM FARM. 1/4 1/8 LF were held up A Coy 1/5 LF assisted 1/8 LF. 2nd Lt STIRRUP with one platoon taking enemy M.G. post at Q5 a 42	

PAGE 5

VOL: 40

Army Form C. 2118.

1/5 LAN: FUS.

WAR DIARY
or
INTELLIGENCE SUMMARY.
(Erase heading not required.)

Instructions regarding War Diaries and Intelligence Summaries are contained in F.S. Regs., Part II. and the Staff Manual respectively. Title pages will be prepared in manuscript.

Place	Date	Hour	Summary of Events and Information	Remarks and references to Appendices
REF 57c SE 1:20000	27/9/18 contd	18.00	Orders were issued for another attack 1/5 L.F. participating, but the attack was postponed	
	28/9/18	02.40	1/4 & 1/8 Lan: Fus. attacked & took objectives on ARGYLE RIDGE	
		03.15	A Coy 1/5 L.F. on left & D on right advanced through 1/4 & 1/8 L.F. & attacked 3rd Objective running N & S through R1 central, behind a creeping barrage	
		04.50	B & C Coys passed through A & D to make good 4th objective along road R2a & c	
		04.45	A boy reported that they went on line R1a 31 – R1c 4.8. Mns was very slow reaching BHQ although prisoners were coming back in large numbers	
		08.00	Communication by telephone was obtained to forward companies	
		09.25	A & D Coys were reported on their objective & in touch with 10th Man on left.	
		12.40	B & C Coys were reported on final objective & were pushing forward patrols. During the afternoon posts were established on railway at R2.b43 & R2 d 48	
		15.00	Batt HQ moved up to Q12 a 45. The 125 Bde were relieved by 2nd New Zealand Bde. Coys moved back to bivouacs in BOAR COPSE area	
	29/9/18	11.00	Battalion moved back to vicinity of BUTLERS CROSS Q3a b & d. BHQ Q4 a 11. Casualties during operations 6 O.R. killed 39 wounded 1 officer missing. Germans captured believed to number 300. 4.77mm 12 Trench mortars 26 Machine Guns captures	
BHQ Q4 a 11	30/9/18		Battalion rested.	

A.S. Castle Lt Col
O/C 1/5 Lanc: Fus

CONFIDENTIAL

WAR DIARY

1/5 LANCASHIRE FUSILIERS

1/10/18 — 31/10/18

VOL. 41.

Army Form C. 2118.

1/5 Lancashire Fusiliers

WAR DIARY
or
INTELLIGENCE SUMMARY.
(Erase heading not required.)

VOLUME 41. Page 1.

Place	Date	Hour	Summary of Events and Information	Remarks and references to Appendices
B.H.Q.	1.10.18		The Battalion was in bivouac in the vicinity of BUTLERS CROSS Q3a & d.	
Q.A.11.	"		The time between the dates mentioned was spent in rest, games, refitting and training. Practice attacks, when the system of companies leap frogging each	
5.10.18			other was employed. Post shooting competitions were carried out during the afternoons.	
B.M.Q.A.11.	6.10.18		A practice attack on BEAUCAMP RIDGE was carried out by the Battalion when the aboves represented a creeping barrage, and the infiltration system was used.	
B.H.Q.A.H.	7/10/18		The Battalion did a practice attack before the G.O.C. a revision of the system of companies leap frogging each other was again used.	
	8.10.18		The third and fourth armies had reached the advance and the 42" Division moved forward to be in support to the N.Z. division. The battalion moved at 11.00 to VILLERS PLOUICH (57 d.S.E) via TRESCAULT & BEAUCAMP and bivouacked for the night	
B.H.Q. R.14.C			in R.14.C.	
B.M.Q. R.14.C	9.10.18		The advance was again resumed and the Battalion had orders to move to (57B.S.W) M.11.C.V.D. with bivouac, from where they would move forward again of the	
M.11.C. (57 B.S.W)			situation permitted. The advance was started at 07.20 from VILLERS PLOUICH and the Battalion	

1/5 Lancashire FUSILIERS. WAR DIARY

INTELLIGENCE SUMMARY. VOLUME 41. Page 2

Army Form C. 2118.

(Erase heading not required.)

Place	Date	Hour	Summary of Events and Information	Remarks and references to Appendices
			marched to NIEVD via BONNET FARM, BONAVIS, VAUCELLES where they halted for 6 hours. At 1605 the battalion again marched to (S7c S.W) N.4.b.4.3.	
B.4.Q			BOUT.DO.PRÉ, via LE BOSQUET, LESDAIN, VESNES and spent the night in billets and bivouacs. One H.V. shell fell in the Battalion area causing casualties.	
N.H.b.h.3			2 killed + 4 (four) wounded.	
	10.10.18		At 1415 the 125 Brigade moved across country via HAUCOURT to FONTAINE.LES-	
B.N.Q			CIRE and the Battalion was billeted in FONTAINES.LES- CIRES R.H.Q at L.15.b.8.6.	
L.15.b.8.6.			The 125 BNF BDE (group) came under the tactical orders of the N.Z. division and had orders to move to squares J.1 + D.25 or it following day.	
R.H.Q	11.10.18		At 1035 the Battalion moved across country to HERPIGNY FARM via LE JEUNE BOIS + HAULCOURT BOIS FARM and was billeted in barn, house and bivouacs.	
D.25.a.5.7.	12.10.18		Maj Ref: 57.B. 4/20,000 The 42nd Div.(two artillery) had orders to relieve the N.Z. division on the line on the night of 12/13 October. D.W. Boundaries SOUTHERN BOUNDARY BRIASTRE CHURCH-	
R.H.Q			BELLEVUE (incl.) E.20.a - E.15.c.0.0. E.15.b.6.0. NORTHERN BOUNDARY QUIEVY.(excl)	
D.22.b.7.3			SOLESMES(excl) At 1600 the Battalion moved from J.25.a and relieved the 2nd Auckland Battalion. The Battalion had two companies holding an outpost line at RIGHT FRONT	

1/5 Lancashire Regiment

WAR DIARY
INTELLIGENCE SUMMARY
(Erase heading not required.)

Army Form C. 2118.

VOLUME "4" Page 3.

Place	Date	Hour	Summary of Events and Information	Remarks and references to Appendices
			Company's "B" LEFT FRON COY, "D" SUPPORT COY and "C" LEADING COY R.H.Q area at D.22.b.7.3.	
			The outpost line consisted of posts noted were dug in on the WEST of the River	
			SELLE on D.18.b.& b. Touch was established on the right flank with /4th R.SCOTS but	
R.H.Q	13.10.18		no where was one touch on the left with the GUARDS DIVISION was on the left flank	
D.22.b.y.3			The Battalion remained unchanged, the enemy shelled our positions severely and caused the following casualties. Officer killed (Capt. Bentley) 10 O.R. killed & 40 O.R. wounded	
			Reconnoitring patrols went out after dark to gain information about the River SELLE and to see whether it was possible to store sufficient bridges. It was found to be 15' wide and from 8'.6. 12' deep and consequence to ford on the Battalion front.	
R.H.Q	14.10.18		The situation remained unchanged until 1400 when 1/6 L.N.L two on our right relieved	
D.22.b.y.3			enemy withdrawing the C.O. sent forward to front line Coy H.Q and Coy Commanders att 1945 1/8 two unfolded having noticed upon E.19.a.23 and a hostile M.G. on railway em- waiting until dark before proceeding further. att 2130 of Coy reported they were across River SELLE and in touch with 1/6 Lo. two about D.18.B.51, all quiet and were moving forward. Brigadier officer had instructions to put a footbridge across River SELLE at D.18.d.2.3. This was duly erected and T.M's took up positions in ravine in D.18.a. to command Bridgehead	

1/5 Lancashire Fusiliers

WAR DIARY
or
INTELLIGENCE SUMMARY.
(Erase heading not required.)

Army Form C. 2118.

VOLUME 41   Page 4

Place	Date	Hour	Summary of Events and Information	Remarks and references to Appendices
			on east of S.O.S. A Coy reported at 2310 K.6. fort established at E.13.C.19 a.m. rifles	
B.H.Q.	15-10-18	0045	fort about D.18.d.77 in touch with 1/5 Lan. Fus. on at D.18.d.3.4 but not in touch with B. Coy on the left A Coy had orders to remain when they were at 2340.	
			B Coy commenced was sent W. of B. Coy that the Guards were on a line D.12.C centres	
D.12.d.7.3		0110	and a platoon was to throw out a flank from D.18.d.1.9 to approximately D.12.a.5.0.	
		0410	B Coy reported in touch with A Coy on right by patrols and communication by telephone established from forward post to various in D.18.a. at Platoon of B Coy were trying to	
			establish posts on Factory road in E.13.a. where going forward they heard sounds of enemy working in Factory in E.13.a. and came across an enemy light machine gun unattended they captured this and withdrew as being about 20 of the enemy afterwards from the Factory.	
			our platoon then withdrew without casualties and established posts just EAST of River	
		0515	SETLE. B Coy reported their output line by post at D.18.b.8.0. (in touch with A Coy at D.18.C.1.9.) D.18.b.90.25 - E.13.a. 0.6 - D.18.D.8.7. The Frank Platoon in posts at D.18.b.66 - D.18.b.5. 9 a.m. touch with Guards at D.12.c.7.5. B Coy were relieved by E Coy before dawn B Coy the incoming support coy. The situation during the day remained unchanged	
On D.22.b.7.3.	16-10-18		The situation during remained unchanged	

Army Form C. 2118.

1/5 Lancashire Fusiliers WAR DIARY

INTELLIGENCE SUMMARY

(Erase heading not required.)

VOLUME 41 Pages

Place	Date	Hour	Summary of Events and Information	Remarks and references to Appendices
R.14.9.	17-10-18.		Before dawn the two front platoons of A Coy were relieved by C Coy. A Coy then became	
D.22 b.1.3			the Coy in support. Casualties 1 OR wounded. The left forward	
			post of outpost line was withdrawn as a shell by our 6" guns fell short at 18.30. on the factory.	
			Immediately after dusk a patrol reconnoitred the factory in E.13.a. and found no enemy there.	
R.14.9.	18-10-18.		Casualties 3 ORs wounded. The situation remained unchanged during the day.	
D.22 b.7.3.			At dusk the Battalion was relieved by 2 Coys of 1/5 East Lancs. and by 1 Coy 1/8 Manchester Regiment. After relief the Battalion marched back to BEAUVOIS EN CAMBRESIS, across country and via JEUNE BOIS, and was in reserve. The night	
I.4.c.4.0			was spent in billets in I.4. (Sheet 57 & N.W.)	
R.14.9.	19-10-18.		During the morning the Battalion bathed and got was issued with a certain amount of new clothing. As the division was resuming the advance on 20-10-18 the Battalion	
A.11.c.0.0			moved at 17.30 to HERPIGNY FARM across country to be there in reserve.	
D.25.c.5.7.	20-10-18.		The Battalion was still in reserve and stayed the day at HERPIGNY FARM.	
R.14.9.	21-10-18.		The 125 Brigade relieved the 127 Brigade in the line. The Battalion moved from HERPIGNY	
D.25.c.5.7.			FARM at 1445 to BELLE VUE F.19.c. via QUIEVY and FONTAINE-AU-TERTRE FARM.	

1/5 Lancashire 4081/1/5/28

WAR DIARY
— of —
INTELLIGENCE SUMMARY.
(Erase heading not required.)

Army Form C. 2118.

VOLUME 41. Page 6.

Place	Date	Hour	Summary of Events and Information	Remarks and references to Appendices
E.20.a.66.			and had dis chge. at 1930. the Battalion went into Brigade support the four companies occupied the road in E.14.b & E.15.c. B.H.Q. were in dugouts at E.20.a.66.	
B.H.Q. E.20.a.6.6	22.10.18		The situation remained unchanged and the Battalion remained in Brigade Sup/port. Ton ammunition with 6.2" howitzer on the left and the 5¨ Jerrerian on the right th	
B.H.Q "	23.10.18		42" Division resumed the advance with th 125 Brigade on the line at 0320. The Battalion was in Brigade support with A & B Coys attached to 1/7 La. two on the right and C & D attached to 1/8 La. two on the left. B.H.Q. moved forward to E.14.central.	
E.14.cen.Cm.A		0100	the four companies moved forward to within about 200 yards of assembly position of the 1/7 & 1/8 La. Fus. A & B. Coys occupied the line of the REAR BROOK in E.15.a & E.9.c. C & D Coys assembled on reverse slope of hill WEST of road in E.3.b.d. & E.9.c. The companies had orders were to advance immediately in rear of the advancing troops and occupy the first objective (line of the road in E.9.d, E.9.b, E.3.d & b.) at 0700 reports were received from companies that they were in position on the first objective at	
		0810	1/7 La. two reported that they were on the final objective (road - E.8.c-E.4.a.) while the 5¨ Division on their right and at QUARRY at E.11.a.3.8. one platoon of A Coy went forward to form a defensive flank from E.5.c.9.6 to E.11.a.3.8. until the 37th Division went strong	

WAR DIARY
of
1/5 Lancashire Fusiliers
INTELLIGENCE SUMMARY. VOLUME 41

Page 7

Army Form C. 2118.

(Erase heading not required.)

Place	Date	Hour	Summary of Events and Information	Remarks and references to Appendices
	23.10.18		the 5th Division at 0840. One platoon of C coy were placed at the disposal of left Coy 1/8 Lan Fus and another platoon of C coy was used by right Coy 1/8 Lan Fus to establish touch with 1/7 R Fus on the night. This was successfully accomplished. the 2 other companies were moving forward at 0005 the enemy put down a barrage on the 5th Division on the right were seen massing for the attack. Our casualties were 2 OR killed 14 wounded. At 0840 the NZ division passed through the 42nd Div and the 37th Division passed through the 5th Division. At 1030 1000 the Battalion had orders to withdraw to VIESLY. The Battalion withdrew at 1230 via BELLE VUE and
B.H.Q			BRIASTRÉ. The night was spent - billets at VIESLY.	
D.28.c.66	24.10.18		At 1046 the Battalion moved back to FONTAINES LES PIRE via AULI COURT FARM JEUNE BOIS	
E.15.b.3.3	25.10.18 & 26.10.18		and were billetted in the village in I.15.b. These two days the Battalion spent in battery and refitting.	
"	27.10.18		There was a Brigade parade when the G.O.C. division (Major General A.S. Ply Peral C.M.G. D.S.O.) presented medals won in the field by officers and other ranks of the 125 Inf Brig.	
"	28.10.18 to 31.10.18		This period was spent in training starting to company and platoon location exercises, ending the morning and recreational training during the afternoons.	

E.M.Critta Lt. Col.
1/5 Lan Fus.

VOLUME 142

WAR DIARY.

CONFIDENTIAL.

1/5 LANCASHIRE FUSILIERS.

1st November 1918. 30/11/18

Army Form C. 2118.

1/5" Lancashire Fusiliers.   WAR DIARY
or
INTELLIGENCE SUMMARY.   VOLUME 42
(Erase heading not required.)   Sheet 1.

Instructions regarding War Diaries and Intelligence Summaries are contained in F.S. Regs., Part II. and the Staff Manual respectively. Title pages will be prepared in manuscript.

Place	Date	Hour	Summary of Events and Information	Remarks and references to Appendices
B.H. at I.15.6. (Sheet 57 B.N.E.)	1-11-18		Capt. L.C. BURN (1/7 Manchester Regt.) joined the Battalion and resumed command. Training was carried out in the morning, and recreational training in the afternoon.	
"	2-11-18		The Battalion did a practice attack under M.G. and L.T.M. to support enemy line ammunition. There was a Brigade cross country run in the afternoon.	
"	3-11-18		There was a Battalion church parade in the morning. During the day there was a Divisional Band contest when the Battalion Band won the first prize contest for the Best Drum and Fife Band.	
"	4-11-18		The 125 Inf/Bde group moved to SOLESMES. The Battalion arrived the starting point, at I.10.b.6.5 (Sheet 57 L(?) N.E.) (at 4.30 a.m.), and marched 6 SOLESMES via BETHENCOURT, VIESLEY, BRIASTRE & BELLE VUE. The night was spent in billets.	
B.H. at P.16.a.8.4. (Sheet 57 L N.W.) & R.30.a.8.7. (Sheet 51 a.S.E.)	5-11-18		The Battalion moved at 0900 hours via VERTIGNEOL thence infantry track W.23.6.9.1. to W.18.L.4.2. The Battalion arrived in billets for the night.	

A/092   W: W1128.9/M1293. 750,000. 1/17. D.D. & L. Ltd. Forms/C2118/14.

1/5 Lancashire Fusiliers.

WAR DIARY
INTELLIGENCE SUMMARY.

VOLUME 42 Sheet 2.
Army Form C. 2118.

Place	Date	Hour	Summary of Events and Information	Remarks and references to Appendices
Sheet 51A S/5 R.H.Q. R.32.a.8.7 Sheet 51 M.36.a.8.2	6-11-18		The 12.5" Inf. Bde group moved to HERBIGNIES. The Battalion moved via road striking N. of LE QUESNOY to R.24.C.4.9. M.12.d.2.5 were formed at M.15.C.04 - VILLEREAU. Companies were billeted in the vicinity of MAISON ROUGE (N.31). The 1.2.5 Inf. Bde group became Bde in support of one hours notice from 1600 hours to the 126 Inf/Bde who were in the line. This Battalion moved to the front to [illegible].	
(Map Ref?) Sheet 51 B.H.Q. N.36.a.8.2 & O.34.a.7.2	7-11-18	0630	C.O. 2nd I/C. O.C. Coy. I/Os. went on a reconnaissance of area in squares O.27.28.33.34: with the view to the Battalion having to defend that area	
		12.05	The Battalion passed the starting point N.31.a.2.8. with orders to proceed to HARGNIES, while on the way the enemy were shelling the village and the situation in general seemed rather obscure. Orders were received to proceed to PETIT BAYAY where the Battalion would billet while further orders were to [illegible] received. Battalion was in billets in O.28 & 34.	
R.H.Q. O.34.a.7.2	8-11-18	1800 0200	C.O. went to Brigade H.Q. to a conference, and returned at 0310.	
		0400	O.C. Coys attended a conference at B.H.Q. when verbal orders were issued for the advance in which the Battalion was to take part. The same day. Conference ended at 0515.	
		0615	The Battalion moved from billets by companies. There were 15 minutes intervals between companies. They went to assemble in P.31.L. where they were to wait until a bridge was built across the	

Army Form C. 2118.

1/5 Lancashire Fusiliers.

WAR DIARY
INTELLIGENCE SUMMARY.

(Erase heading not required.)

VOLUME 42
Sheet 3.

Instructions regarding War Diaries and Intelligence Summaries are contained in F.S. Regs., Part II. and the Staff Manual respectively. Title pages will be prepared in manuscript.

Place	Date	Hour	Summary of Events and Information	Remarks and references to Appendices
As on Ref. Sheet 31.	8-11-18	0615	river SAMBRE at somewhere in P.32 or V.5. While on the way there information was received that the bridge could not be taken in time. No orders were issued for companies to take the following new Road in O.35, V.5, crossing the SAMBRE at V.5.d.9.3. through PATIGNY, along the road N. of BOIS GEORGES, and along the road in V.8.a. Then they were to assemble along the WEST of the railway from P.33.a.8.3 to P.33.d.7.8.	
B.H.Q. O.34.a.4.2.				
B.H.Q. P.31.d.5.8		0930		
"		1100	Left Coy (D) Right Coy (C) were formed up between P.33.a.8.3 & P.33.d.7.8, ready for sending out patrols. C.O. left A.H.Q. to see the Coys form up and to see the patrols go forward.	
		1130.	A platoon from D & C Coys left and right, respectively were forward to occupy the line of the road from P.35.a.9.9 to P.33.c.7.8.	
		1150	A & B. Coys were formed up about about 200 yards behind the remainder of D & C. Coys waiting to go forward when the first objective was reached.	
B.H.Q. P.33.a.8.2.		1245.	B.H.Q. advanced to P.33.a.8.2.	
B.H.Q. P.33.a.8.2.		1310.	D & C. Companies were on the 1st objective. D coy in touch with 1/4 Lan. Fus. on the left at P.36.a.9.9. There was no touch with 5th Division on the left of D Coy but right of C. Coy. B Coy were getting into position on the right of C. Coy.	

WAR DIARY or INTELLIGENCE SUMMARY

Army Form C. 2118.

1/5 Leicesters. VOLUME 42. Sheet 4.

Place	Date	Hour	Summary of Events and Information	Remarks and references to Appendices
Map Ref. Sheet 51. O.H.Q. P.33.a.8.2.	8.11.18		continue the advance for the final objective i.e. the line of the MAUBEUGE - AVESNES road from P.26.a.2.3 to P.31.d.8.3) together with D&C. Coys.	
		13.15	A. Coy went forward to take over the first objective. 1/4 Leic. & us on our left were through the BOIS de POSSNOY (P.28.2 & 35) and were in P.2.8.a.	
		13.40	Patrols from the three forward Coys i.e. B, D & C. went forward to make good the final objective and encountered slight machine gun fire from P.30.a, FORT D'HAUTMONT.	
		14.20	The enemy heavy shelled the first objective for a few minutes (Rafales) by a Sgt. who was wounded thro'.	
		14.25	1/7 La. & us were hung up by M.G. fire from P.30.a.	
		15.10	I.O. went forward from B.H.Q. to first objective to obtain information about the right and centre companies.	
		16.30	The companies were trying to push forward. Situation approximately was. Outpost line ran from P.33.8.0.0 to P.36.c.7.8. Enemy machine gun fire from FORT D'Hautmont and Larme at Lovet.	
		18.30	Rt. coy was held up by M.G. fire from the Larme at Lovet and they tried to surround it.	
		18.20	orders were issued to B. Coy (left Coy) to push ahead and try & take Fort D'Hautmont.	
		19.05	Rt. Coy (——) Fort D. Hautment and Larme at Lovet were taken by left and Rt. Coys.	

Army Form C. 2118.

1/5 Lancashire Fusiliers.

WAR DIARY
of
INTELLIGENCE SUMMARY. VOLUME 42.

Sheet 57.

(Erase heading not required.)

Instructions regarding War Diaries and Intelligence Summaries are contained in F. S. Regs., Part II. and the Staff Manual respectively. Title pages will be prepared in manuscript.

Place	Date	Hour	Summary of Events and Information	Remarks and references to Appendices
(Mat Ref.? Sheet 51)	8-11-18	1905	Artillery without opposition	
		2000	Rd. Coy. Hqrs moved to same as 7 inst.	
B.H.Q.		2330	A. Coy withdrawn from first objective to road in V.4.A.4.7 where they were bivouacked in homes.	
P.23.a.9.2.		2200	The three forward coys went forward to make good the objective.	
	9-11-18	0500	At day break... Day also Lorrie reports had been received that all coys had taken their forward objectives and were occupying same. Patrols had been pushed out and it was believed that the enemy had withdrawn as the front was exceedingly quiet and no sniping or M.G. fire was taking place.	
		0600	C.O. went forward and established a defensive line. B. left front, C. Rt. front, D. support coy and A coy: reserve. On the first objective. It was definitely established that the enemy had withdrawn as one of our patrols had advanced 4 miles but saw no signs of the enemy.	
		0900	Bn. put the cavalry through & took - lined with the enemy.	
		1100	B.H.Q. moved to same as 7 inst.	
Q.31.a.1.3.		1600	1/7 La. F. on right and the Dominions front were established in outpost line. This Battalion moved into HAUTMONT and billets. Coys were met by the band and cheered by civilians who cheered and carried	

Army C. Forms/C2118/14

Army Form C. 2118.

WAR DIARY
INTELLIGENCE SUMMARY.

(Erase heading not required.)

1/5 Lancashire Fusiliers.

VOLUME 42   Sheet 5

Instructions regarding War Diaries and Intelligence Summaries are contained in F.S. Regs., Part II. and the Staff Manual respectively. Title pages will be prepared in manuscript.

Place	Date	Hour	Summary of Events and Information	Remarks and references to Appendices
In the Field {Sheet 57} B.M.Q.	9-11-18		Training today.	
P.29.C.6.7.	10-11-18		The day was spent in cleaning up and resting. I.O. went forward at enemy outpost line & found that the situation the enemy was having a hard time. B.M. + C.O.s and O.C. [illegible]	
		10.0pm	A wire was received that hostilities would cease at 1100 that day. Orders were that troops in their present positions.	
		10.45	Rev. was ordered and the C.O. made a speech. The chanted pipers of the Brigade filed the "Crane fair, no Parade" merry. The Battalion gave three cheers for the "Queen and Victory".	
	11-11-18	11.00	They were the ceremonies for the day.	
	12-11-18		The Battalion spent the day in training and recreation training in the afternoon.	
			Training was carried out in the morning and recreational training in the afternoon. It was learnt that Lieut. [illegible] was killed in an [illegible] offensive. In the afternoon a memorial service was held at Francais who had died at HAUTMONT during the war this was attended by representatives of all ranks and a great number of civilians. There was music by Lieut. A. H. Bowman of [illegible] and organist, was [illegible] after a short service.	

WAR DIARY or INTELLIGENCE SUMMARY

Army Form C. 2118

1/5 Lancashire Fusiliers.

VOLUME 42. Sheet 7.

Place	Date	Hour	Summary of Events and Information	Remarks and references to Appendices
(M4 Rd? 31 but 51) B.H.Q. P.29.c.6.7.	14.11.18		The day was spent in training and recreational training	
	15.11.18		C & D Coys together with other representatives of the Division were to on parade when two German guns, captured in HAUTMONT by the 1/5 Manchester Regt, were presented to the town of HAUTMONT by the Division (42nd). Recreational training was carried out in the afternoon.	
	16.11.18		Training was carried out during the morning and recreational training during the afternoon.	
	17.11.18		There was a Battalion church parade - the square of the town in the morning and recreational training in the afternoon.	
	18.11.18		There was a Battalion route march in the morning. Route BILLETS - LES GRAVETTES - FERRIERE-LA-GRANDE - road junction @ 29.a.2.6. - FORT BOUR DIAU - FORT D'HAUTMONT - BILLETS. There was recreational training during the afternoon & interior economy was done in the evening in men's billets.	
	19.11.18		Training during the morning and recreational training during the afternoon was carried out.	
	20.11.18 to 21.11.18		A fatigue party of 3 N.C.O.s and 150 O.Rs was found by the Battalion daily, each company in turn, (1 N.C.O. and 15 O.Rs) for finding fatigues at Divisional and Corps HAUTMONT. Training during the morning and recreational training in the afternoon was carried out by companies with no fatigues.	

Army Form C. 2118.

WAR DIARY
INTELLIGENCE SUMMARY.
(Erase heading not required.)

1/5 Lancashire Fusiliers. VOLUME 42. Sheet 8.

Place	Date	Hour	Summary of Events and Information	Remarks and references to Appendices
{And Ref. Sheet 51. 1/40,000} B.H.Q. P.29.c.6.7.	23/11/18		From 0930 to 1230 the Battalion did a route march of 7 miles. Route Béihl - ?ame to WARGNORIES - FONTAINE - LIXMONT FONTAINE - V.23.a.9.7 - ST REMY MAI BATN - V.20.4.9. Recreational training was carried out during the afternoon.	
"	24-11-18. 24-11-18.		There was a Battalion Church parade in the morning and recreational training in the afternoon. Capt. S. North joined the Battalion from Hospital & Capt. C.H.C. Munt from England.	
"	25/11/18		During the cool weather the Battalion spent the day cleaning and completed one officer and 30 O.Rs. worked under R.E. supervision at Q.14.a.3.8 from 0345 to 1200 hours.	
"	26/11/18.		The Battalion with 1st Line transport took part in a Brigade route march from 0936 to 1245 hours. Route O30 b.4.3 - L6.5 GRAVETTES - LOOBROIL - ST LAZARE - Q.9 central - 20th Roman Q.17.c.4.3. FERRIERE Q.22.b.9.3 - Q.23.c.4.8 - T roads Q.29.c.2.6 - cross roads Q.26.a.3.3 - 20.17 D. Wacincourt. Distance 8 miles. A party of one officer and 30 O.Rs. worked under R.E. supervision at Q.14.a.3.8 from 0345 to 1200 hours.	
"	27/11/18		The morning was spent in firing and general training. Recreation training was carried out during the afternoon. A party of 1 officer and 30 O.Rs. worked under R.E. supervision at Q.14.a.3.8. 2-Lt. W. Stringer proceeded to England.	
"	28.11.18	0930	Battalion paraded for C.O.'s inspection and were afterwards dismissed for general cleaning of kit and equipment. Owing to inclement weather	

Army Form C. 2118.

WAR DIARY
INTELLIGENCE SUMMARY.

1/5 Lancashire Fusiliers.

VOLUME 42.
Sheet 9.

Place	Date	Hour	Summary of Events and Information	Remarks and references to Appendices
Map Ref Sheet 51. B.H.Q. P.29.b.6.7.	29.11.18.		Lewis gun training, firing and training were carried out during the morning. Battalion training was carried out during the afternoon. 1 officer and 60 O.R. rejoined from 0600 & 1200 hours under R.E. Superannum at Q.14.a.3.8.	
	30.11.18	0932	Battalion proceeded the Starting point C.35.a.9.4 for a route march. Route C.35.a.9.4 - FONTAINE V.11.a.1.4 - LIMONT FONTAINE V.17.a.5.2 - V.23.c.7.6 - V.24.a.4.1 - CHURCH ECLAIBES - V.24.a.2.4 - X Roads W.13.d.3.0 - BEAUFORT W.14.a.8.9 - W.14.c.6.8 - W.8.a.4.3 - W.14.c.4.1 - Q.31.b.9.3 FORT D'HAUTMONT. BILLETS. Distance 8 miles at maathey 140 9 18 officer and 200 O.R. marched from 0200 & 1800 hours under R.E. Superannum at Q.14.a.3.8. Recreational training was carried out during the afternoon. Lt. F. St. BARBE joined the Battalion from 1/5 Bn. Lenvision Regt.	

Greg Ahern
Major
Commanding 1/5 Lancashire Fusiliers

SECRET.

Copy No.

1/5th. BN. LANCASHIRE FUSILIERS.

OPERATION ORDER NO. 45.

Ref. Map 57 B. 1/40000.   3/11/18.

(1).   The 125th. Infantry Brigade Group will move to SOLESMES on 4/11/18.

(2).   STARTING POINT - Main Road, I.10.b.6.5. This unit will pass same at 1300 hours 4/11/18.

(3).   ROUTE - BETHENCOURT - VIESLY - BELLE VUE.

(4).   Battalion will parade on Battn. Parade Ground, facing "C" Coy's. H.Q. by 1000. ready to move by 1215. Dress:- Full Fighting Order, blanket horseshoe fashion round haversack.
Four markers per Company will report to RSM. on parade ground at 1200

(5).   OFFICERS' VALISES, will be dumped at respective Compy. H.Qrs. by 1000. T.O. will arrange to collect.

(6).   MESS BOXES, will be brought to B.H.Q. by 1130.

(7).   TRANSPORT.
(a). First line Transport and Baggage Wagons will accompany the Batt:
(b). Coy. L.G. Limbers will be sent to respective Coy. H.Qrs. at 0930 loaded and returned to Transport Lines.
(c). Mess Cart will report to B.H.Q. at 1130, be loaded and then returned to Transport Lines.
(d). All Transport will be loaded, formed up under orders from T.O and ready to move by 1225.

(8).   O.C. Coys. will ensure that their respective Coy. areas are left in a clean and sanitary condition; windows and doors closed and all furniture stored inside buildings.
Certificates to this effect will be handed to Adjutant on parade.

(9).   ACKNOWLEDGE.

Capt. & Adjutant.
1/5th. Lancashire Fusiliers.

Issued at 2200 thro' Sigs.
Distribution:-
Copy No. 1. "A" Coy.
         2. "B" Coy.
         3. "C" Coy.
         4. "D" Coy.
         5. "H.Q."
         6. T.O. and Q.M.
         7. Adjt. & File.
         8. War Diary.

SPECIAL ORDER OF THE DAY

by

Major-General A. SOLLY-FLOOD, C.M.G., D.S.O.
****

The success of anoth Division to-day amounts to over 2,000 prisoners, 40 guns, and a great advance through difficult country.

It may be bad to "better", but, if it is possible to do so I am confident that you will "better" it.

Give them your best, and good luck to you.

Signed. A. SOLLY-FLOOD.

Major-General.
Commanding 42nd. Division.

4th. Nov. 1918.

SECRET. COPY NO ...8...

1/5TH. BN. LANCASHIRE FUSILIERS.

OPERATION ORDER NO.46.
****

Ref.Maps 51.A. S.E. & 57.B. N.E. 1/20,000. 5/11/18.

(1)   The 125th.Inf.Bde.Group will move to-day 5/11/18 to BEAUDIGNIES or, if BEAUDIGNIES is occupied by the 127th.Inf.Bde.Group to VERTIGNEUL-PONT-a-PIERRES Area.

(2)   If Bde.Group does not move further than VERTIGNEUL - PONT-a-PIERRE Area, this Battn. will remain in the vicinity of PONT-A-PIERRES.

(3)   STARTING POINT. Road junction E.Q.c.3.3. This Unit will pass same at 0800 hours 5/11/18.

(4)   ROUTE. Cross Roads R.4.b. - VERTIGNEUL - thence Infantry will use track W.23.b.9.1. to W.18.b.4.2. Transport will move via crossroads W.23.d.9.2. thence by W.17.c.1.2..

(5)   The Battn; will parade in column of route on right of road in front of B.H.Q. facing North in the following order:-
    H.Q.Coy., Band, 'A', 'B', 'C' & 'D' Coys.
Head of Column to rest at R.7.a.8.5. All to be in possition, ready to move, at 0730 hours. Dress:- Same as for O.O.No.45 3/11/18.

(6)   OFFICERS VALISES. will be dumped at Q.M.Stores by 0600 hrs.

(7)   MESS BOXES. will be brought to B.H.Q. by 0645 hours.

(8)   TRANSPORT.
  (a) 1st Line Transport & Baggage Wagons will accompany this Bttn.
  (b) Mess Cart will report to B.H.Q. at 0645 hours, beloped and then return to Transport Lines.
  (c) All Transport will be loaded, formed up under orders from T.O. and ready to move by 0730 hours.

(9)   LOADING. will be carried out by H.Q.Coy. under supervision of R.S.M.

(10)   "Marching-Out" States, together with "Clean" Certificates will be handed to Adjutant on parade.

(11)   ACKNOWLEDGE.

Capt. & Adjutant.
1/5th.Bn.Lancs.Fusiliers.

Issued at 0110 thro' Sigs.
Distribution as for O.O.No.45.

G.54.

SECRET.

To:-
   O.C.
      Companies & H.Q.
      T.O. & Q.M.
      Adjt. & File.
      War Diary.

WARNING ORDER.

(1)   Ref. Warning Order G.47 and continuation G.52 of yesterday, at 0600 hours to-day, 7/11/8, 62nd. Division on left are advancing from BROWN LINE with objective HARGNIES – Bois DELGAVE Road.
      126th. Inf. Bde. are conforming by advancing their left on HARGNIES and road South of Village to Cross Roads O.29.b.
      When HARGNIES is captured patrols are exploiting towards VIEUX MESNIL.

(2)   125th. Inf. Bde. Group will be prepared to move forward at 0600 hours to-day.
      This Battn. will move off first and will be prepared to pass the Starting Point at 0630 hours. Starting Point, cross roads MAISON ROUGE N.31.a.3*3* All arrangements will be made at once to enable this to be done; men breakfasted, etc., etc.

(3)   Coy. Lewis Gun Limbers, and two Limbers for H.Q. only will accompany the Battn.
      Further orders will be issued later with regard to the remainder of transport

(4)   ACKNOWLEDGE'

                                              Capt. & Adjutant.
Issued at 0115 thro' Sigs.   1/5th. Bn. Lancs. Fus.
7/11/18.

SECRET.   COPY NO...8....

1/5th. BN. LANCASHIRE FUSILIERS'

OPERATION ORDER NO. 48.
****

Ref. Map. Bt S.W. 1/20,000.   7/11/18.

(1)   125th. Inf. Bde. Group will move to OBIES to-day.

(2)   STARTING POINT. MAISON ROUGE, N.31.a.3.7. This unit will pass same at 1205 hours.

(3)   ROUTE. Will be notified later.

(4)   Companies will be on parade at Company Alarm Posts, ready to move off, at 1200 hours.
        H.Q.Coy. and Band will move off from their Alarm Post to vicinity of MAISON ROUGE, reaching there by 1200 hours.
        Order of March:- H.Q.Coy., Band, 'A', 'B', 'C' & 'D' Coy.

(5)   OFFICERS VALISES, MESS BOXES, ETC., will be sent to Transport Lines and Q.M. Stores forthwith.

(6)   TRANSPORT. 1st Line Transport will be accompany the Battn. also Baggage Wagons.
        All necessary arrangements will be made by T.O. to enable him to be ready to move at 1200 hours.

(7)   LOADING. Will be carried out by H.Q.Coy. under supervision of R.S.M.

(8)   DRESS. Same as for O.O.No.45 3/11/18, excepting that S.B.Rs will be worn at the 'Alert'.

(9)   ACKNOWLEDGE.

                                                    Capt. & Adjutant.
Issued at 1130 thro' Sigs.   1/5th. Bn. Lancs. Fus.
Distribution as for O.O.No.45.

G.52.

SECRET.

To:-
O.C.
Companies & H.Q.
T.O. & Q.M.
Adjt. & File.
War Diary.

URGENT.

(1)   In continuation of Warning Order G.47 of to-day, 125th Inf. Bde. will be prepared, if ordered, to occupy BLACK LINE? i.e., road from N.36.c.0.0. via FORRESTER'S HOUSE to N.12.d.1.0., tonight as follows:-
1/5th.Lan.Fus. from Southern Divl.Boundary to Road Fork N.30.a. 7.3. (inclusive)
1/7th.Lan.Fus. from this Fork (inclusive) to Northern Boundary.
1/8th.Lan.Fus. along road on West edge of Forest between Divisional Boundaries.

(2)   This unit will be prepared to occupy positions as under:-

'B' Coy....Southern Divl.Boundary to FORRESTER'S HOUSE(inclusive)
'C' " ....FORRESTER'S HOUSE (exclusive) to N.30.c.7.0.
'D' " ....N.30.c.7.0. to Road Fork N.30.a.7.3. (inclusive)
'A' " ....Support. Approximately along LAIE AUPEPIN N.29.b.
Location of Battn.H.Qrs. will be notified later.

(3)   In the event of the above move taking place tonight, O.C.Coys. and I.O.(mounted) will meet the C.O. at FORRESTER'S HOUSE at 0600 7/11/18 and reconnoitre forward areas as far East as BROWN LINE, i.e., main road East of Forest from LA CHAUSSEE O.15.d. to PONT-sur-SAMBRE U.11.a.
Should move not take place tonight, they will meet the C.O. at the same time and for the same purpose at MAISON HOUSE.

(4)   Acknowledge.

Capt. & Adjutant.
1/5th. Bn. Lancs. Fus.

6/11/18.

SECRET.   COPY NO....8....

1/5TH' BN. LANCASHIRE FUSILIERS.

OPERATION ORDER NO. 47.
****

Ref. Maps 51A. S.E. & 51 S.W. 1/20,000.   6/11/18.

(1)   125th Inf. Bde. Group moves to HERBIGNIES to-day 6th. inst.

(2)   STARTING POINT. Cross Roads R.33.a.65.30. This unit will pass same at 0800 hours.

(3)   ROUTE. Road skirting North of LE QUESNOY to L.44.c.4.9. - M.12.d.8.8. - cross roads M.15.a.6.4. - VILLERRAUD
                                                    right
(4)   The Battn. will parade in column of route on road/of road in front of B.H.Q. facing South in the following order:-
           H.Q. Coy., Band, 'A', 'B', 'C' & 'D' Coys.
Head of column to rest opposite B.H.Q. All to be in position ready to move at 0745 hours.
Dress:- Same as for O.O.No.45, 3/11/18.
Usual distance will be maintained throughout.

(5)   OFFICERS VALISES. will be dumped at Q.M. Stores by 0615 hrs.

(6)   MESS BOXES Will be brought to B.H.Q. by 0700 hours.

(8)   TRANSPORT'
           (a) First Line Transport and Baggage Wagons will accompany the Battalion.
           (b) Mess Cart will report to B.H.Q. at 0700 hours, be loaded and then return to Transport Lines.
           (c) All Transport will be loaded, formed up under orders of T.O., and ready to move by 0745 hours.

(8)   LOADING. will be carried out by H.Q. Coy. under supervision of R.S.M.

(9)   'Marching Out' States, together with 'Clean' Certificate will be handed to Adjutant on parade

(10)   ACKNOWLEDGE'

                                                    Capt. & Adjutant.
Issued at 0400 thro' Sigs.   1/5th. Bn. Lancashire Fusiliers.
Distribution as for O.O.No.45.

SPECIAL ORDER OF THE DAY

by

Major-General A. SOLLY-FLOOD, C.M.G., D.S.O.

*********** *******

The Armistice proclaimed to-day has brought the operations in which the Division was engaged to a premature conclusion.

Generally speaking, the recent fighting was not of the violent nature in which you have previously taken part and so greatly excelled. At the commencement of the operation, however, it was sufficiently severe and the conditions imposed by the Forest of MORMAL and the bridgeless River SAMBRE were such as to call for the highest soldierly qualities.

After long marches at night in bad weather over boggy forest tracks, although cold and wet, hungry and tired, you attacked and defeated the enemy with your customary indomitableness.

When the history of the war is written your efforts commencing in the Forest, when forcing the passage of the bridgeless River SAMBRE in the face of severe enemy fire, and culminating in the capture of the Town of HAUTMONT, will rank very high among the exploits of soldiers during this great war.

I consider that the Divisional Motto has once again, probably for the last time, been entirely upheld.

Officers, N.C.O's and men of all arms and services in the Division I am proud to be your Commander and to be able once more to thank you ; in the name of our King and Country, for your gallant deeds and your steadfast loyalty.

Signed. A. SOLLY-FLOOD.

Major-General,
Commanding 42nd Division.

11th Nov., 1918.

WO 23

Poole 41.8.
15 sheets

CONFIDENTIAL.
WAR DIARY.

VOLUME 43. / DECEMBER 1916
                31   "   "

1/5. LANCASHIRE FUSILIERS.

Army Form C. 2118

WAR DIARY or INTELLIGENCE SUMMARY

VOLUME 43.

1/5 Lancashire Fusiliers.   1/5 Sheets.

Place	Date	Hour	Summary of Events and Information	Remarks and references to Appendices
Mf Rf Sheet 51 G.N. 9 P. 29.C.6.7.	1-12-18		His Majesty the King inspected the 42nd Division. The Battalion lined the Eastern side of the MAUBEUGE-AVESNES road from Q.20.a.8.7 Southwards. At 1110 hrs H.M. the King arrived at cross roads Q.20.a.8.7 where he met the G.O.C. Division and Brigadier General. He then walked along the road which was lined by troops of the Division, and was cheered as he passed along. Recreational training was carried out during the afternoon.	
	2-12-18	0930 & 1230.	Battalion aid a rout march. Route. Billet.- P.20.a.8.7 - 2.B.9. - H.Q.12.c.52 - Q.12.a.4.4. - CHURCH MAUBEUGE - Q.2.a.4.4 - Q.1.a.52 - P.6.3.9.1 - P.12.c.5.2 - P.22.a.8 - P.25.a.8 - BILLETS. Battalion offrs & 9 miles. During the afternoon the finals for the Platoon (Knock-out) Competition were won by 2 Platoon A Coy. No.8 Platoon B coy were the runners up.	
	3-12-18		2 N.C.O's went on billeting fatly to the new area. The Battalion paraded for C.O's inspection of Coy HOT stores, mens equipment, Lewis guns, Coy & Platoon Pack Horses, & Bombs, A.B. 439 etc. Owing to inclement weather a Battalion route march was cancelled. General cleaning of Lewis guns, equipment was carried out during the morning.	
	4-11-18			
	5-12-18	0930 & 1300 hrs	Battalion moved for a route march. Route. BILLETS - L'AGACE - VIEUX MESNIL - LES CHEMINS - FERME DE LA FOSSE - BOUSSIERES - BOIS D'HAUT MONT - P.27.a.15.90 - BILLETS. Distance approx 9 miles. Recreational training was carried out during the afternoon.	
	6-12-18		During the morning training (firing on the ranges, close order & ceremonial drills, rapid loading) was carried out. Recreational training was carried out during the afternoon.	
	7-12-18		During the morning training (firing on the ranges, close order) was carried out. No.2 Platoon A Coy fought a platoon of 1/8 Lan 3us & claimed best platoon in the Brigade. Result No.2 Platoon the winners. Report 1/5 L.F. 1 goal. 1/8 L.F. Nil.	

LT. F. ST. BARRE, 2nd M.T.R. STARKEY. SMITH, C.Q.M.S. T.E. ACTON M.M. 200012, Sgt. A. MOONEY 200035 & Sgt. E. SMITH. V.C. D.C.M. 51396 proceeded to ENGLAND to fetch Regimental colours from the Drill Hall BURY.

1875 Wt. W593/826 1,000,000 4/15 J.B.C. & A. A.D.S.S./Forms/C.2118.

WAR DIARY or INTELLIGENCE SUMMARY

Army Form C. 2118

1/5 Lancashire Fusiliers

VOLUME 43 Sheet 2.

Place	Date	Hour	Summary of Events and Information	Remarks and references to Appendices
Map Ref } Sheet 51 } B.It.Q. P.2.Q.b.b.	8-12-18.		Battalion attended Church Parade in the morning. Officers & W.O.s and Sgts. Mess of A.Coy played the V.R. of their Coy. Runners 4-0 for O.Rs. 2 NCOs W. Rae Crear and 2 B.O.R. proceeded to NAMUR to take over a guard from the Canadians of war material captured by the Germans.	
	9-12-18.		Battalion spent the morning in training (firing, drill, etc). A/ex U.R. of Battalion was used for inspection and inoculated during the morning. Remainder training. Remainder training men paraded and during the afternoon.	
	10-11-18.		The morning was spent in training (firing, drill, etc). Owing to inclement weather and being too ventilated no sports were carried out during the afternoon.	
	11-12-18.		Battalion which 1st time transport x-roads P.30.b.4.4. was parades at 0922 hours and went to Q.26.a.2.2. P.31.b.9.4 where at the main point owing to heavy rain the Battalion returned to Gilles.	
	12-12-18.		The morning was spent in training & lectures. Owing to inclement weather no sports were carried out during the afternoon. The officers annual 1st OR paraded to CHARLEROI to clean up billets.	
	13.12.18.		The Battalion spent the morning in training and the afternoon in recreational training. but transport	
Map Ref } Sheet 9/10 ams VALENCIENNES 51.H.45.3.B. Map Ref NAMUR 1/10 map B.H.Q. 2.B.25.80.	14.12.18	1125.	The Battalion recommenced the march to CHARLEROI and went via LOURDIL to MASBREUGE FAUX or MONS where they spent the night in billets.	
	15/12/18	0932	The Battalion resumed the march and went via VILLERS-SUR-NICOLE ½ mile South of + GIVRY thence to ESTINNES AU MONT where they spent the night in billets.	

1/5. Lancashire Fusiliers

WAR DIARY or INTELLIGENCE SUMMARY.

Army Form C. 2118.

VOLUME 43
Sheet 3

Place	Date	Hour	Summary of Events and Information	Remarks and references to Appendices
Map Ref. M+MJR 1/10,000 B.H.Q. 2 B.25.8.0	16.12.18	0917	The march was again resumed and the Battalion went into BINCHE to ANDERLUES where they spent the night in billets.	
2.D.3.76	17.12.18		The day was spent in resting and cleaning up preparatory to the march into CHARLEROI	
"	18.12.18	0917	The Battalion finished the march going by the main MONS - CHARLEROI road and arrived at CHARLEROI at 1,330 hours. The weather was very bad, a rain fire continuously during the march. The Battalion was sent into the Belgian Infantry Barracks for billets.	
2 F 35.93	19.12.18		The day was spent in cleaning and organization of Barrack rooms etc. required a certain amount of work there spending in them. The colour party which went to Bury to fetch the Battalion Colours arrived back to the Battalion.	
"	20.12.18		The day was again spent in cleaning and organization of the barracks.	
"	21.12.18		The Battalion did a ceremonial parade first to receiving the colours.	
	22.12.18		The Battalion attended church parade in the morning after that parade the Battalion paraded in close column of companies previous the colours. Before the	

WAR DIARY or INTELLIGENCE SUMMARY

Army Form C. 2118.

1/5 Lancashire Fusiliers

VOLUME 43
Sheet 4.

Place	Date	Hour	Summary of Events and Information	Remarks and references to Appendices
Ref. Ref. Sheet NAMUR 1/100,000 G.H.Q. 27 35 93	22.12.18		Colours were brought on parade the Battalion moved into line and saluted them as they were brought on parade. The Battalion afterwards marched past by companies at columns distance and formed a hollow square into which the colours were brought and the C.O. made a speech giving the history of both the colours and the Battalion. The colours were then escorted to the officers mess where they were left. 110 O.R. proceeded to England to be demobilized.	
	23.12.18	0930-1130	This time was spent in training and the remainder of the day was spent in decorating dining hall for Christmas. 130 O.Rs proceeded to England to be demobilized. When the Battalion was on Brigade duty, Barrack guard of 1 N.C.O and 12 men, guard of 1 N.C.O. and 3 men over material left by the enemy on tracks on the railway near CHARLEROI station and approximately 1 coy for various fatigues, the mentioned was found from this unit. In addition a piquet of 1 officer and 20 Rs patroled the streets of CHARLEROI from 1800 hours to 2200 hours. The piquet was composed of a civilian disturbance so an enlying piquet of 3 officers and 100 o.Rs armed and supplied with ammunition stood in readiness to turn out if any disturbance took place.	
	24.12.18		A believe was given on the forenoon 3 cheers to be best by the C.O. the remainder of the day was spent in preparing for Christmas. Battalion was on Brigade duty. 100 Rs proceeded to England to be demobilized.	

WAR DIARY or INTELLIGENCE SUMMARY

Army Form C. 2118.

1/5 Lancashire Fusiliers.   VOLUME 43   Sheet 5.

Place	Date	Hour	Summary of Events and Information	Remarks and references to Appendices
Bing 2 F: 35. 93. Sheet 1 NAMUR 1/100,000	25.12.18		There was a Battalion Church Parade in the morning. The G.O.C. inspected all Coy dining places & judged the best decorated in the Division. B Coy was adjudged best decorated in the 125 Bde. At 1600 hours the men had their Christmas dinners when the officers and Sgts acted as waiters. Div.	
	26.12.18		The day was observed as a general holiday except that the Battalion was on Brigade duty.	
	27.12.18		The morning was spent in training and a party of 1 officer and 25 others were employed in making a rifle range. 4 O.Rs proceeded to England to be demobilised. The Battalion was on Brigade duty. A lecture was given at 0930 hours "under the educational scheme. The Battalion attended a lecture on 'Reconstruction' in Italia" in Town.	
	28.12.18			
	29.12.18		There was a Battalion church parade in the morning. Major F: GREY BURN M.C of this Battalion went to NAMUR as Brigade Field officer to inspect guards found by the Brigade on ammunition and material seized by the enemy.	
	30.12.18		In the morning there was a memorial parade at memorial service organized by the civil authorities was held in the Church at 1000 hours and subsequently the 3/5 race cemetery at CHARLEROI. Infantry Barracks CHARLEROI. "In memory of those soldiers and civilians who died = CHARLEROI during enemy occupation as a result, either directly or indirectly, of enemy action. The Battalion lined the left side of the street from the Church to Cemetery. Battalion was on Brigade duty.	

1/5 Lancashire Fusiliers.

WAR DIARY
INTELLIGENCE SUMMARY.

Army Form C. 2118.
VOLUME 43
Sheet 6.

Place	Date	Hour	Summary of Events and Information	Remarks and references to Appendices
Maf Ref Sheet MANOR 1/100, 000 Bt 9.2.F.35.93	3/12/18		The morning was spent on Education, men taking various subjects from formal under the instructor for the subject., 0930-1230 4 classes of French Reading, writing & arithmetic were held. Instruction being formal from within the Battalion. Recreational training was carried out during the afternoon.	
			Battalion strength advisory with Battalion 1-12-18. 29 officers. 530 R.R.	
			Rejoined from hospital, leave & courses — 31	
				29 561.
			Proceeded on leave courses, hospital & demobilised 3 41	
			Strength on 31-12-18. 26 520	

RCCatto. Lt. Col.
Commanding 1/5 Lancashire Fusiliers
31-12-18.

SECRET.   1/5th. BN. LANCASHIRE FUSILIERS ADMINISTRATIVE INSTRUCTION

No. 1.

Issued in connection with 1/5th. Battn. Lancs. Fus. OPERATION ORDER
No. 49, a/d. 13/12/18.

Ref. Map 1/100000. VALENCIENNES & NAMUR.

1. **BILLETING.** Billeting area for each day is shown in attached Appendix "A"

When vacating present billets, special attention will be taken to ensure that all billets are left in a thoroughly clean, and sanitary condition. Where unoccupied houses are being used, all windows and doors will be closed prior to vacation.

Each day Rear Parties will be left behind to settle up previous nights billets, and clean up where necessary. This party to consist of one man per company and 2nd. Lieut. Brooks.

Advanced billeting parties as under will report to the Staff Captain Brigade H.Q. at 0730 hours, on the mornings of the 14th, 15th, 16th, and 18th. inst:-

Capt. L.B. Dean, and 1 N.C.O. per Coy. who can cycle.

The Signal Officer will provide bicycles.

The same Advance Party will be detailed each day. The officer of each party will be prepared to state ration strength of his unit, for that day. This officer will be mounted.

Billet returns will be rendered to Battn. Orderly Room by 1800 hours daily.

2. As the comfort of the men is the first consideration, additional transport for blankets, will remain with the unit throughout the march.

REFILLING POINTS. Appendix "A" shows the Refilling Point of the Brigade Group each day. Any alteration or addition, will be notified when necessary.

Supply wagons will refil at 0730 daily, and will rejoin the respective units transport, under the charge of units representatives, in time to proceed to the line of march.

HORSE RUGS. Throughout the march it is probable most animals will have to stand in the open. It is therefore essential that every animal that has been clipped should be provided with a horse rug. Horse Rugs for draught animals will be carried on vehicles to which the animal is attached. Horse rugs for riders must be distributed amongst the units transport - no special vehicle can be provided for the purpose.

Issued through Brigade at............

Lieut. & A/Adjutant,
1/5th. Lancashire Fusiliers.

Copy No. 1. to C.O.
2. to Adjutant.
3. to S.O.
4. to H.Qrs.
5. to A. Coy.
6. to B. Coy.
7. to C. Coy.
8. to D. Coy.
9. to P.O.
10. to Quartermaster.
11. to Billeting Officer.
12. to Rear Party Officer.
13. to R.S.M.
14. War Diary.
15. File.

Copy No. 14

APPENDIX "B" TO OPERATION ORDER NO. 49.

During the forthcoming move only Zero hour will be notified to companies, upon which action will be taken as under. By this means it is hoped to save valuable time in issuing orders.

Zero hour.	Hour at which Battalion will be formed up on Alarm Post on right of road facing starting point ready to move off in column of route (Band in threes) in the following order:- "H.Q" - Band - "A" - "B" - "C" - "D" - & Transport.
Z - 15 mins.	Chargers to be at B.H.Q., Coy. H.Qrs., etc.
Z - 45 mins.	Horses report to Coys. for Cookers. Mess Cart to B.H.Q. Maltese Cart to Aid Post. All Coy. Mess Boxes to be ready for loading at B.H.Q.

Z - 60 mins.	All blankets, Officers' valises & Drummers' packs to be dumped at loading point, which will be notified with Zero hour.
	    Breakfast under Coy. arrangements, but to be in time to allow the above to be carried out.
	    Dinner will be cooked on march, and issued on arrival in billets.

0700 hours.	REVEILLE.

Blankets will always be rolled in bundles of ten, securely tied at both ends and labelled by Coys. They will be re-issued under supervision of R.S.M. "H.Q" Coy. will find loading and unloading parties.

Copy No. /4

APPENDIX 'A' TO OPERATION ORDERS NO....

All Map Refs., unless otherwise stated are 1/100,000 Sheet 12 & 8.

DATE.	STARTING POINT.	HOUR PASSING STARTING POINT.	FROM	TO	ROUTE.	REFILLING POINT.	REMARKS.
Dec.14th.	Road Junction ¼ mile South of first 'O' in LOUVROIL.	1202	HAUTMONT.	MAUBEUGE FAUBG de MONS.	LOUVROIL.	-	No. Unit to move L. of HAUTMONT BRIDGE FORT HAUTMONT Head before 1115.
Dec.15th.	Road Junction ¼ mile EAST of last 'S' in LES PASSES. LA BANLIEUE.	0932 1000	MAUBEUGE!	ESTINNE AU MONT.	VILLERS SURE NICOLE. Pts.10 ½ mile South of GIVRY.	MAUBEUGE Sheet 51. Q.3.a.3.8.	
Dec.16th.	Cross Roads 1 mile N. of 'A' in ESTINNE AU MONT.	0917.	ESTINNE AU MONT.	ANDERLUES'	BINCHE.	ESTINNE CHURCH.	
Dec.17th.			HALT	FOR	DAY.	ANDERLUES. 23 Kilo post.	Coal may be drawn from Refilling Point at ANDERLUES on 16th & 17th inst. Fuel will be carried for 14th & 15th.
Dec.18th;	Cross Roads ¼ mile N.E. of 'T' in ANDERLUES STA.	0917.	ANDERLUES.	CHARLEROI.	Main MONS CHARLEROI Road.	as above.	

COPY.   COPY NO. 64.

1/5TH. BN. LANCASHIRE FUSILIERS.
OPERATION ORDER NO. 50.

14/12/18.

(1) REVEILLE............0630.
(2) ZERO................0830.
(3) ALARM POST.........."D"Coy.Billets.
(4) PARADE in column of route facing East in the following order :-
    Cyclists - "D"Coy - Band - "C" Coy - "B" Coy. - "A" Coy.
    "HQ"Coy. and Transport.

(5) LOADING POINTS. Battn.H.Q. & "A"Coy..... Q.M. Stores.
                    "B","C" & "D" Coys...... At respective Coy.HQ.

(6) REAR PARTY parade at Battn.HQ. at 0800.

(7) Orderly Officer for tomorrow :- 2/Lieut. F.MOUNTFORD.
    Next for Duty :-   Lieut. L.A.CALDWELL.
    Company on Duty tomorrow :-   "D" Company.
    Next for Duty :-   "A"   -do-

                                    (sd.) F.P.Quigley,
Issued at 1745 hours.   Lieut. & A/Adjutant.
Distribution as per O.O.49.   1/5th Lancashire Fusiliers.

1/5TH. BN. LANCASHIRE FUSILIERS.   COPY NO. 1.

ADDENDUM NO. 1 to O.O. NO. 50.

14/12/18.

1. STARTING POINT will be - Road Junction at M. of MAUBEUGE and not as in Appendix 'A'.

2. This unit will pass Starting Point at 0900 hours.

3. In future Cooks marching with Cookers will wear Fighting Order. Their packs, covered up, will be carried in the crate.

4. SICK PARADE............0640.

Sgd. R. R. QUIGGIN.
Lieut. & A/Adjutant,
1/5th. Bn. Lancashire Fusiliers.

Issued at 1745 hours.
Distribution as per O.O. No. 50.

1/5TH. BN. LANCASHIRE FUSILIERS.   COPY NO.....

OPERATION ORDER NO. 51.

                                                                     16/12/18.

1. REVEILLE.....................0630.

2. ZERO HOUR....................0855.

3. ALARM POST................... 'D' Coy. Billets.

4. PARADE in column of route, head of column facing EAST, in the following order:-
Cyclists - 'D' Coy. - Band - 'C' Coy. - 'A' Coy. - H.Q. - 'B' Coy.
Transport in Square facing main road.

5. LOADING POINT........Bandstand in Main Square by Church.

6. Q.M. details and men surplus to Transport will march with Battn. H.Q. and not in rear of the baggage waggons.

7. Orderly Officer for tomorrow :- Lieut. L. A. Caldwell.
    Next for Duty :- 2nd. Lt. J. Atkinson.
    Company on Duty tomorrow :- 'A' Company.
    Next for Duty :- 'B' "

(Sgd) ....
Lieut. & A/Adjutant,
1/5th. Bn. Lancashire Fusiliers.

Issued at 1700 hours
Distribution as per O.O. N° 50.

COPY NO.........

1/5TH. BN. LANCASHIRE FUSILIERS.

OPERATION ORDER NO. 52.

17/12/18.

1. ROUTINE.   Reveille...............0630.
   Sick Parade............0645.
   Orderly Officer for to-morrow:- 2nd.Lt.J.Acton.
   Next for Duty:-   2nd.Lt.H.Hargreaves.
   Company on Duty to-morrow:- 'C' Coy.
   Next for Duty:-   'D' "

2. ZERO HOUR.............'B' Coy. 0915. ALARM POST....Point 25.
   Head of Column Cross Roads facing North.
   Zero Hour............0905 - Battalion, less 'B' Coy..
   Alarm Post...........Cross Roads by 'A' Coy.
   Head of Column - Cross Roads facing NNE. in following order:- Cyclists, Drums, 'A', 'C', 'D' & B.H.Q.

3. LOADING POINT.............Company Headquarters.
   H.Q. at Q.M.Stores.

Lieut. & A/Adjutant.
1/5th. Bn. Lancashire Fusiliers.

Issued at   Hours,
Distribution as per O.O.NO.50.

CONFIDENTIAL 9824

WAR DIARY.

1/5th LANCASHIRE FUSILIERS

VOLUME 44. 1ST JANUARY 1919
31ST

H.2.A.
6 sheets

Army Form C. 2118.

WAR DIARY
INTELLIGENCE SUMMARY.
(Erase heading not required.)

1/5 Lancashire Fusiliers. VOLUME 44 Sheet 1.

Place	Date	Hour	Summary of Events and Information	Remarks and references to Appendices
NAMUR 1/100,000 C.H.935.93			When the battalion was on Brigade duty the following duties were found. 2N.C.Os and 100 Rs for barrack guard. 3 officers and 1000 for inlying piquet, who stood by in barracks ready to turn out to quell any riots which might occur during their 24 hours of duty in CHARLEROI. A piquet of 1 officer and 30 O.R. to patrol the streets of CHARLEROI from 1600 hours to 2000 hours.	
	1-1-19		The morning was spent in training (arms drill & examination drill). A working party of 1 officer and 250 Rs were employed in making a rifle range. Recreational training was carried out during the afternoon. Battalion was on brigade duty.	
	2"		The morning was spent in education when the Battalion subjects taken were Reading, Writing, Arithmetic, French, English History, Tyfewriting and Shorthand.	
	3"		The Battalion paraded for a route march. Route RUE du PONT NEUF, SOUTHERN bank of Derivation canalise BRIDGE over railway west of CHARLEROI STN, BEAUMONT road, MONT SUR MARCHIENNE LATOMBE to road junction 400 yds S of VIN CAILLOU, there small circle and back to CHARLEROI by same route. Distance 8 & 9 miles. 2nd Lt Atkinson and 290 Rs proceeded to NAMUR to relieve 2nd Lt Mc Crae and 29 Ors who were guarding ammunition (in th CIT ADELLE there) held by the enemy. Battalion was on brigade duty	

1/5 Lancashire Fusiliers

WAR DIARY
INTELLIGENCE SUMMARY
(Erase heading not required.)

Army Form C. 2118.

VOLUME 44 Sheet No 7

Place	Date	Hour	Summary of Events and Information	Remarks and references to Appendices
Map Ref NAMUR 1/100,000 13.14.9 CHARLEROI 27.35 9 3	4-7-19		Educational classes were held within the Battalion during the morning. No 2 Platoon A Coy played a section of the M.G. Batn in the first round of the Divisional Inter Platoon Knock out competition. Result No 2 Platoon 4 goals M.G.Bn 0.	
	5/7		There was Battalion Church Parade. No morning and recreational training was carried out during the afternoon.	
	6/7		C Company was employed in making a rifle range and the remaining 3 companies carried out training. No 1 Platoon A Coy played No 1 Platoon 1/10 Manchester Regt. for the Semi final and won by 2 goals to 1. The following were awarded of ribbons of Capt. S.M. NORTH MILITARY CROSS. 235488 C.S.M. H.R.W. WATSON. D.C.M. & 5558 Sgt. T. LEEMING. DISTINGUISHED CONDUCT MEDAL. Battalion was on Brigade duty.	
	7/7		Educational classes were held within the Battalion during the morning. Recreational training was carried out during the afternoon.	
	8/7		The battalion spent the morning in training (musketry, arms & ceremonial drill). No 2 Platoon A Coy played No 1 Platoon the 1/6 MANCHESTER Regt. for the final. Result No 2 MANCHESTER Regt 4. No 2 Platoon consequently were the second best Platoon in the Division.	

1/5th Cameron Highlanders

Army Form C. 2118.

VOLUME 44
Sheet 3

WAR DIARY
or
INTELLIGENCE SUMMARY.
(Erase heading not required.)

Place	Date	Hour	Summary of Events and Information	Remarks and references to Appendices
CHARLEROI	9-1-19		Educational classes were held within the Battalion during the morning. Recreational training carried out during the afternoon. The Battalion was on Brigade duty.	
	10th		The Officers and O.Rs not employed on duties and fatigues spent from 09.30 to 11.00 in firing on the range. The Battalion attended a lecture by Lt C.D NAPIER on "CAUCASUS AND ITS PEOPLES". Recreational training was carried out during the afternoon.	
	11th		Educational classes were held within the Battalion during the morning. Battalion played the 1/8 R.S? at rugby football and beat by 15 (?) to 6 NIL.	
	12th		There was a battalion church parade in the morning. Recreational training was carried out during the afternoon. Battalion was on Brigade duty.	
	13th		The Officers and O.Rs who were sick or on duties and fatigues spent the morning in firing at the range. Recreational training was carried out during the afternoon. Lt A.W.R. MUNRO, S.N.C.O and 3 O.Rs proceeded to England for demobilization	
	14th		Educational classes were held within the Battalion during the morning. Recreational training was carried out during the afternoon. R.H. Coy Lt TONGUE, 5 N.C.O's and 11 O.Rs proceeded to be demobilised in Scotland. Owing to inclement weather a Brigade route march was cancelled. The Battalion spent the morning in barracks in weekly lectures and trench mortar and lewis gun	
	15th		instruction. Battalion was on Brigade duty.	

WAR DIARY or INTELLIGENCE SUMMARY

Army Form C. 2118.

1/5th Lancashire Fusiliers.   VOLUME 44   Sheet 4.

Place	Date	Hour	Summary of Events and Information	Remarks and references to Appendices
NAMUR Map Ref GHQ CHARLEROI 2F.35.93	16/1/19		Educational Classes were held in the Battn Barracks, + a lecture was given on the "Nouveau Theatre" by Major BECKWITH SMITH DSO. Subject: "The Naval Raid on ZEEBRUGGE". 120 all ranks attended. 2 OR proceeded to UK for Demobilisation. "The PIVOTAL PIERROTS" (the Bn concert party) gave their opening performance in the Barracks at 1830.	
	17/1/19		The morning was occupied in general cleaning up of equipment etc for Major General's inspection. A lecture was given by Rev. W.O. JENKINS. Subject "SOUTH AFRICA". 120 all ranks attended.	
	18/1/19		Brigade Parade on Champ de Manoeuvre for presentation of following by G.O.C. 42nd Div. the following from this Battn were among the recipients. 2nd Lt A CALDWELL M.C., CSM CARLESS D.C.M., Sgt O. LEEMING D.C.M. + Pte STEATHAM M.M. A lecture was given by Lt Col APLIN D.S.O. on DEMOBILIZATION & RECONSTRUCTION. 120 all ranks attended. Capt DERN Demobilised.	
	19/1/19		Battn Church Parade, + a concert given by the Durnt Orchestra in the "Universite du Travail".	
	20/1/19		Brigade Commander's Inspection of Battn + Barracks. 21 Officers + 416 OR were on parade, followed by 2nd Cmdr EVERAD, RN on the "Submarine" illustrated with slides. 120 OR attended.	
	21/1/19		Educational day. In the afternoon Soccer Match versus 8th LF. Final 5th LF 3 goals 8th LF 1.	
	22/1/19		Musquetry & Sphestice on range. 2 cmd Lt WHITWORTH + 7 OR proceeded to UK for demobilisation.	

1/5 Lancashire Fusiliers

WAR DIARY
or
INTELLIGENCE SUMMARY.

VOLUME 44
Sheet 5

Army Form C. 2118.

Place	Date	Hour	Summary of Events and Information	Remarks and references to Appendices
Map Ref NAMUR 100,000 B+Q 27 35.93	23/1/19		Educational Day. 26 OR proceeded to UK for Demobilization	
	24/1/19		Batln bathed. 200053 RQMS. EARNSHAW. J. awarded MSM in New Year's Honours	
	25/1/19		Educational Day & lecture in honour of leading in "Empire Returns" kindly by Capt GUEST, 12.0 all ranks attended. The Batln. won 125th Bde Cross Country Race	
	26/1/19		Batln attend Church Parade in Eden Theatre. 10 OR proceeded to UK for demobilization	
	27/1/19		morning occupied in cleaning barracks. 2 OR to UK for Repatriation. 240 30?	
	28/1/19		Sgt BERRY (old No 1251 NFS) awarded MSM in New Years Honours. Educational Day. 235043 CSM. F.J CARLESS, DCM. "A" Coy died in 20 ccs of pneumonia completed	
	29/1/19		Coys at disposal of Coy Commander for cleaning barracks. CSM CARLESS buried at FLUY; 10 OR	
	30/1/19		Educational Day; 2nd Lt W. McBRAE + 27 OR proceed to UK for demobilization	
	31/1/19		Batln bathed	

Rey Amm Major
Comdg. 1/5 Bn Lancs Fus.

1/5 Lan Fus.
War Diary 1st Feb. 1919
            28th "   "
Vol 45

43.B.

1/5 Lancashire Fusiliers VOLUME #5 Sheet 1.

Army Form C. 2118.

WAR DIARY
INTELLIGENCE SUMMARY.
(Erase heading not required.)

Place	Date	Hour	Summary of Events and Information	Remarks and references to Appendices
BHQ MARSAY NUMBER 100000 2F 85.93	1.2.19		Educational Classes held in Barracks. Lecture in "Norman Theatre" by Mr W.H ROBERTS on "Measuring" Drawing & Sketching etc" 4 Officers + 60 OR attended	
	2.2.19		Church Parade Services.	
	3.2.19		Infantry Training on Champs de Manouevres: Capt & QM BUSSEY & 39 OR proceeded to UK for demobilization	
	4.2.19		Educational Classes held in Barracks. Lecture in "Norman Theatre" by Rev E.D MARTIN on "Leagues of Nations" 4 Officers 60 ORs attended	
	5.2.19		Companies employed in cleaning up Barracks: 20 ORs proceeded to UK for demobilization + 5 OR demobilised whilst on leave	
	6.2.19		Educational Classes held in Barracks: 3 OR's taken on strength from Base: Capt B. HOWE evacuated sick to BOR: + 2 hush of strength	
	7.2.19		Company Bathed & cleaned Barracks: During competition held in Barracks in afternoon by S. HOWDEN + 15 OR proceeds UK for Demobilisation: 3 or demobilising whilst on Leave	
	8.2.19		Educational Classes held in Barracks. 4 ORs demobilised whilst on leave	
	9.2.19		Church Parade. 23 ORs proceed to UK for Demobilisation	

WAR DIARY

1/5 Lancashire Fusiliers

Army Form C. 2118
VOLUME 45 Sheet 2

Place	Date	Hour	Summary of Events and Information	Remarks and references to Appendices
Map 10J NAMUR 1/100,000				
BHQ 2F 35 93	10.2.19		Battn (less draft of 6 offrs + 130 OR) moved into Billets at MONCEAU-SUR-SAMBRE. (BHQ 2 F 73 95). in order to hold to staff the W barn for Concentration Camp; 15 ors of the bodyguard of the transport personnel were also left at CHARLEROI. Capt CHELTNUT + 9 OR proceeded to UK for demobilization. Battn now organised with one Coy 'C' consisting of 4 platoons A B C D find Party under Lt CLARKSON + 80 ors attached to IV Corps Concentration Camp for duty	
	11.2.19		remainder Battn spent day in cleaning up new billets	
	12.2.19		Draft Coy occupied in Inspection of Kit etc & cleaning up Barracks	
	13.2.19		ditto	
	14.2.19		Bathing Parades & Inspection for Draft Coy	
	15.2.19		Bathing, Cleaning up Barracks & billets	
	16.2.19		Church Parade & Eden Theatre	
	17.2.19		The Draft Coy moved from CHARLEROI, & joined Battn at MONCEAU-SUR-SAMBRE 2nd Lt ACTON + 15 men of Cadre, & the transport personnel remaining at CHARLEROI	
	18.2.19		Coys employed in cleaning up billets etc. 2/Lt STRINGER + 27 ors proceeded to UK for demobilization; 2 OR demobilized in UK whilst on leave.	
	19.2.19		Draft Coy carries out IT Sec 5. 9 ors attd 1/2 5 Inf/Bde demolished	

1/5 Lancashire Fusiliers

WAR DIARY
or
INTELLIGENCE SUMMARY.
(Erase heading not required.)

Army Form C. 2118.
VOLUME 45
Sheet 3

Place	Date	Hour	Summary of Events and Information	Remarks and references to Appendices
NAMUR / DUTOUR BHQ 2 ETB 95	20/2/19		Draft 60 spent morning having kits inspected: Lt Col CASTLE MC assumed command of the Battn. 16 ORs demobilised: 10 r joined from leave & taken on strength	
	21.2.19		Boys marched to Baths at CHARLEROI for Bathing. All mobilisation stores were put in room at Infantry Barracks CHARLEROI for purpose of checking, preparatory to the Cadre returning to the U.K.: 4 ORs demobilised	
	22.2.19		Draft had kits inspected, & cleaned billets: 6 ORs demobilised	
	23.2.19		Church Parade in Hôtel de Ville MONCEAU: 84 ORs demobilised	
	24.2.19		Draft 60 spent morning doing I.T. & Recreational Training. Major F.J. Burn MC proceeded on leave	
	25.2.19		Draft spent morning doing Military Recreational Training	
	26.2.19		do 2 Cpl STROOD "G" died in 20 CCS from Influenza	
	27.2.19		do	
	28.2.19		Draft marched to CHARLEROI for Bath: the Battn were runners up in the Bde Group Football Gross tournament, winners being Hdqrs R.H.Q.	

A.S.Castle Lt Col
1/5 Lancashire Fusiliers

Vol 26

War Diary
16th Lanc⁵ Fusiliers
1ˢᵗ MARCH 1919
31ˢᵗ "

VOL 46

1/5th Lancashire Fusiliers

Instructions regarding War Diaries and Intelligence Summaries are contained in F.S. Regs., Part II. and the Staff Manual respectively. Title pages will be prepared in manuscript.

Army Form C. 2118.

VOLUME 46
Sheet 1

WAR DIARY
or
INTELLIGENCE SUMMARY.
(Erase heading not required.)

Place	Date	Hour	Summary of Events and Information	Remarks and references to Appendices
Map Ref. MAHVR 1:100000 BK12 2.E 7:25	1-3-19		Voluntary Church Service. Summer Time came into use at 23.00 hours.	
	2-3-19		Military & Recreational Training.	
	3-3-19		Do. Belgian currency was the only one in the country.	
	4-3-19		Military & Recreational Training. 2 O.R. demobilized on leave.	
	5-3-19		Military & Recreational Training. 2 O.R. to England for demobilization. FRANCS 5 fr = 3/10 GERMANY - 5 MARKS BELGIUM 5 fr = 3/9 HOLLAND - 2 GULDEN
	6-3-19		Baths at Charleroi. Rate of Exchange	
	7-3-19		Coys at disposal of Coy Comdrs. Baths at Charleroi	
	8-3-19		Voluntary Church Services. 15 OR to England for Demob.	
	9-3-19		Military & Recreational Training.	
	10-3-19		Military & Recreational Training.	
	11-3-19		Baths. 2 OR demobilised on leave	
	12-3-19		Military & Recreational Training. Baths at CHARLEROI	
	13-3-19		— do — & training at Batln	
	14-3-19		& training at Batln. 1 O/R of RE COMP EMC proceeded to UK to rejoin his permanent Unit. 1 O/R Royal Warwickshire Regt	

1/5th Lancashire Fusiliers

VOLUME 46
Sheet 2

WAR DIARY
or
INTELLIGENCE SUMMARY
Army Form C. 2118.

Place	Date	Hour	Summary of Events and Information	Remarks and references to Appendices
CHARLEROI Map 1/100,000 Sheet 43. 96	15/3/19		Military & Recreational training	
	16/3/19		Voluntary Church Services. 3 ORs proceeded to UK for demobilization & 20 ORs UK to join their (regular battalions)	
	17/3/19		Military & Recreational training	
	18/3/19		do	
	19/3/19		2nd Lt A CHARNLEY, 2nd Lt A J BOORNE + one OR proceeded to UK for demobilization. 5 ORs proceeded to UK to join their regular battalions.	
	20/3/19		Bath at CHARLEROI + Military training. 2/Lt A J OSBORNE proceeded to UK for demobilization. Lieuts G.R. ALLEN + E RILEY. 2nd Lts W TILL + J H CLARKSON proceeded to GERMANY to join 15th Battn L'AN FUS. 18 ORs struck off strength on proceeding to join 15th Bn LAN FUS on standing of leave	
	21/3/19		Bath at CHARLEROI. Military & Recreational training	
	22/3/19		Church parade Apres in Town Hall MONCEAU-SUR-SAMBRE. 3 ORs proceeded to UK to join their Regular Battn	
	24/3/19		Military & Recreational training	
	25/3/19		do	

1/8th Lancashire Fusiliers

VOLUME 46 Sheet 3

Army Form C. 2118.

WAR DIARY
or
INTELLIGENCE SUMMARY.
(Erase heading not required.)

Instructions regarding War Diaries and Intelligence Summaries are contained in F.S. Regs., Part II. and the Staff Manual respectively. Title pages will be prepared in manuscript.

Place	Date	Hour	Summary of Events and Information	Remarks and references to Appendices
Map ref NAVIA 1:100,000 BHQ. Q.F. 73 95	24/3/19		Baths at CHARLEROI	
	27/3/19		Military Recreational Training:	
	28/3/19		— do — & Baths at CHARLEROI	
	29.3.19		Military Recreational Training: 5 OR proceed to UK for demobilization	
	30.3.19		Voluntary Church Services — CHARLEROI. a/Capt Haywood M.C. & 1 OR proceed to CHARLEROI on demobilization	
	31.3.19		Draft by motors to Infantry Base to CHAR-LEROI in order to load Motor Stores on vehicles, preparatory to the entrainment of the CADRE.	

SECRET.   COPY NO. 14

                    1/5th. BN. LANCASHIRE FUSILIERS.
                    OPERATION ORDER NO. 40.

Ref. Sheets 12 & 8 1/100000.   13th. December, 1918.

1.   The Battalion will march to CHARLEROI, commencing December 14th.
in accordance with Appendix "A".

2.   Detailed orders in connection with move are given in Appendix "B".

3.   The comfort of the troops will be the first consideration during the
march.
     Marching out States will be handed to Adjutant on parade. daily

4.   S.A.A. to be carried on the man during the march will be reduced to
60 rounds.

5.   DRESS. (a). Full marching order. Caps will be worn, and steel helmets
carried against the back of the pack by means of the supporting straps.
Mess tins will be carried below the pack. Box respirators will be carried
on top of the pack, waterproof sheets showing below the flap of the pack.
Greatcoats in pack, jerkins will not be carried.
     (b). Transport Drivers will wear jerkins, and haversacks on
back in place of packs. Greatcoats strapped in front of saddle.
     (c). Bands and Transport Drivers will carry steel helmet slung
from left shoulder strap. Mounted officers will carry steel helmet
attached to saddle.

6.   MARCH DISCIPLINE. The provision of 4th. Army No. G.S.128 will be
strictly adhered to; special attention being paid to the following points:-
     1. During halts, chargers and pack animals must be well on
the right hand side of the road, with their heads facing in towards the
road.
     2. Rear parties of 6 Other Ranks under an Officer will
march immediately in rear of the transport of each unit; this party
will be responsible for clearing the road of any broken vehicles, etc.
and generally ensuring that the road is not blocked for units in rear.
This party to be found by the Coy. on duty daily.
     3. Men left behind in billets, or for any purpose, will be
properly marched under an officer or N.C.O.
     4. When marching at ease, the rifle will be slung on either
shoulder.
     5. In order to give space on the road, bands will march in
sections of threes and not in sections of fours.
     6. DISTANCES. Will be as laid down in above mentioned Letter
with the following additions:-
          Between unit and its Transport   50 yards.
          Between sections of Transport   50 yards.

7.   First line Transport will accompany units on the March; baggage,
blanket, and supply wagons of the Train will march with 1st. Line
Transport.
8.   As soon as possible after arrival in Billeting Area; Coys., Q.M.,
and T.O., will send one orderly who knows their own H.Qrs. to report to
B.H.Q., and take back with him a B.H.Q. runner to find the way.

9.   All references in orders, and reports will be to the 1/100000 map.

10. A watch will be circulated to all companies each evening, while
on the march, with correct time.
Marching in States will be rendered to B.O.R. by 1600 hrs daily
     Issued at........... through Signals.
                                                    Lieut. & A/Adjutant,
                                                    1/5th. Lancashire Fusiliers. P.T.O

Copy No. 1. to C.O.
2. to Adjutant.
3. to S.O.
4. to M. Gun.
5. to A. Coy.
6. to B. Coy.
7. to C. Coy.
8. to D. Coy.
9. to T.O.
10. to Quartermaster.
11. to Billeting Officer.
12. to Rear Party Officer.
13. to R.S.M.
14. War Diary.
15. File.

www.ingramcontent.com/pod-product-compliance
Lightning Source LLC
Chambersburg PA
CBHW080851230426
43662CB00013B/2073